The Complete Guide To Success In Real Estate Sales

By

Larry Hauser

ISBN: 0-7596-8767-6 (e-book)
ISBN: 0-7596-8768-4 (Paperback)

This book is printed on acid free paper.

1stBooks - rev. 11/22/02

IN DEDICATION

I would like to dedicate this book to the two individuals who actually helped me to "put it in writing."

The first is Ray Felton, actor, from Leesburg, VA, who convinced me that it would be the right thing to do if I shared what I knew about sales with others who had not had the experiences I had had. It was Ray who told me that a lot of people could benefit from my knowledge and experience if I would just take the time to put it into written form and then deliver it. He told me, while we were sitting in a little Western style restaurant in that little hamlet of Leesburg, that there were literally thousands of people trying to make it in the Real Estate business who did not have a clue about what it was like to "sell" something. What they needed was what I had: knowledge. So, my hat's off to Ray for giving me that vote of confidence and the little push I needed to get going on my project.

The other person is Joseph David Lee. J.D. to all who know him. Perhaps the best sales person I have ever known personally, it was J.D. who taught me the way to converse with people in the FAB way. I first met J.D. as a salesman at a large furniture retail chain, and was consistently amazed at how he could convince people to buy furniture from him, at that time, at that place, at that price. A truly amazing individual who went on to Real Estate sales and then into a very lucrative catering business. To this day, he is probably convincing people that his catering service will provide the absolute best and tastiest food for their parties or functions, and that further investigation of other catering services would be absolutely pointless. The consummate sales person, J.D. taught me that if you believe in yourself, it's easy to convince people of the same.

Wherever these two guys are today, I hope that someday I'll be able to shake their hands and thank them personally.

TABLE OF CONTENTS

INTRODUCTION

The book which you are about to read could be called an instruction manual in salesmanship. There has never been anything like it made available in written form. It is based on the simple premise that a TRAINED salesperson will, over the long run, be more successful in the Real Estate business than an UN-TRAINED sales person. If you agree with that premise ... read on. If you do not agree with that premise, you should put this book back on the shelf and select another book to read.

What you will find in this book is a compilation of information, which I have composed into a format that is detailed, and complete and it is something I have worked on getting into written form for a long time. What I have done for this project is to illustrate what I have learned in my many years in the selling business and relate to you, the inquisitive reader, what **WORKS**, and what **DOESN'T WORK** in various sales situations. I don't have any hocus-pocus secret remedies for success. I have heard of many, and so probably, have you. But, be advised: there are none. There are no "Three Steps to Instant Success." There are no "Secret" marketing plans.

I will discuss proven methods of selling, which are *SPECIFIC* - and which you can write down and tailor to your own personalities and styles. Over time, if you use these methods, you *WILL* improve your SELLING SKILLS so that you will be more effective in what you do. In essence, you will become PROFICIENT AT SELLING and learn how to STOP WASTING TIME. If that sounds like a good program, continue on. However, before you begin, let me express this to you the diligent reader: even if you learn what NOT to do in sales situations by reading this book, you will have gained some very valuable knowledge. For example: if you learn how to recognize my *FOUR TRAPS TO GUARANTEED FAILURE* and how to skillfully avoid them in your listing presentations, how much time and money have you saved yourself? How much is one deal worth to you?

So, in your analysis of whether or not to purchase and read this book, ask yourself these two questions, "How much is it worth to me to make one or two more deals each year that I work in the Real Estate business?" "How much is it worth to me to reduce my WASTED time?" Your answers will determine your decision regarding the purchase of this book.

Writing a Book On Selling

I began to think about writing this book a few years ago when I was telling a friend of mine from back East, Ray Felton, about a fellow who had come into my office in Palos Verdes, California to sell a seminar on *"How To Become The Master of Your Own Life,"* or something like that. We talked about the various individuals we had known about over the years who were offering seminars. You have probably heard from the same ones: Mike Ferry, Tommy Hopkins, Tony Robins, Zig Ziglar, and many others whom I can't recall. Most of them were good, and certainly all had something to offer. But I realized that I had never heard anyone offering a seminar specifically designed for **"Selling Real Estate."**

You Don't Sell Until You Are Trained.

And yet, when I was in the corporate world, *every single* company I worked for had a sales training program for their salespeople and those salespeople **would not go out into the field until they had completed the sales program**. Why is that? And furthermore, of the dozens of Real Estate offices around town, only a *very few* have *Sales* Managers, much less *Sales Training*. Think about that! Most offices have *Office* Managers, not *Sales* Managers. All the sales positions I had in the corporate world provided me with a *Sales Manager*. What's up with that?

In Real Estate, they give you a desk and a phone, and tell you to "Go get 'em." It really doesn't make sense. Is there anyone reading this far who can give me a logical reason why so many Real Estate companies don't have **Sales Trainers** and **Sales Managers**? Well, I can tell you why------------it's because they don't have to. That is just how the Real Estate business is. Agents are independent contractors and therefore, if they want training, it is up to each individual to get whatever training they think will be most beneficial to them.

Most Real Estate Brokers, generally speaking, have nothing, or very little, invested in their agents. Real Estate companies do not operate like IBM, where the hiring of new people is very selective. And when these new people are hired by these large companies, several thousands of dollars are invested in TRAINING these people to sell the company's products. In Real Estate, if a new agent can sell one or two properties during the year, that's good news for the broker. But if another agent comes along who can sell three properties, guess what?? The agent who sells two properties each year gets to "work at home" and the other agent gets the desk. That's business, folks.

"I Lose One or Two Deals Every Year."

Ask yourself the question: "How much business do I lose every year because I did not ask the right questions?" After you have left your meeting with your prospects, you can't go back and re-present. Most people will agree, your best chance of success when you sit down with prospects is your first chance. So, it is a reasonable statement when I say that a skillfully and properly prepared presentation to either buyers or sellers has a much higher probability of success than one presented in a haphazard manner. You are competing against a lot of very successful people who have been in the Real Estate business for a long time. And those people have learned, through their own trials and errors, and *TRAINING*, how to be *"SALES"* people.

In the Real Estate business, what you have at your disposal for marketing tools are not that much different than what your competitor has. So, how do you prosper or, *even survive*, in the tough business of Real Estate sales?

The answer is: persistence and skills. **SALES** skills. The two go hand in hand. A *trained sales person* is always persistent and coordinates that attribute with sales skills. Without **PERSISTENCE** *and* **SALES** skills, you will see many deals get away which were yours for the taking. If you agree with my statement that missing a deal in the Real Estate business is expensive, both in time and money, you may continue on.

Myself - How Did I Start?

When I was only 13 I got my first sales job. I sold Christmas cards, door to door, in the summer, in Ocean City, New Jersey. I sent away for the catalog and order forms from the Christmas card company, picked out a neighborhood, and walked from house to house, asking people if they would be interested in buying some Christmas cards. I had absolutely no training.

FACT: *People Buy If They Think It Benefits Them To Buy.*

I didn't know anything about **SALES** at that age, but I believed in my product. Also, I discovered something, just by dumb luck, which is the ***ESSENCE OF SALES***: **people buy things if they think it benefits them to buy it**. Now that is a rather elementary statement, wouldn't you agree? So, the opening line that I developed after only about 10 or 12 tries, was: *"Hi. My name is Larry. Do you do a whole lot of shopping around Christmas time?"* Of course, the answer was usually "Yes." My **LEAD QUESTION** was one I was certain would be answered in the affirmative. My next question was: *"Well, I have a great idea how you can avoid shopping for one really important thing around Christmas time. Wanna see?"* My second question was one that a "reasonable" person would also answer in the affirmative, because naturally, a person would want to know how to save time around Christmas. Wouldn't you agree, there is never enough time around Christmas to get everything done?

This job was a great introduction for me to the life of a sales person. I was learning how to interact with people and get them to think my way - that is: buy some Christmas Cards in July and August!!! WOW!

FACT: *People Buy From People They Like.*

Another valuable fact that I discovered from my little Christmas Card initiation period was: *people buy from people they like.* Rarely, will anyone ever buy from someone they don't like. So, I always had a smile. People with smiles are happy, and happy people are easier to like. I'm sure you'll agree.

Later, after college, I was involved in the selling of many things. I've been a stock broker for a member firm of the NY Stock Exchange, I've sold life insurance for a large life insurance company, sales representative for Petersen Publishing Company of Los Angeles for several years, long term health care insurance for GE Capital in Newport Beach, etc., etc. But, my favorite of all is Real Estate Sales.

So, in this book do not expect to see an outline of how to do productive farming in specific neighborhoods. Do not expect to see instructions on how to make successful cold calls. Do not look for methods of successful marketing plans. Those must be found elsewhere. In this book you will learn how to develop and enhance your SELLING skills, and by doing this you will, at the same time, learn how to STOP WASTING TIME. With information you will obtain from this book you cannot help but to increase your income and increase the enjoyment you receive from your chosen profession: Real Estate Sales.

I

What Is *Real* Selling?

PERSUASION

So, what is *REAL* selling? **REAL selling is a step by step procedure, of first defining the need, then providing solutions for fulfilling that need, which if *followed in order*, will ultimately result in your prospect agreeing with what is necessary to make a decision to buy that solution from you.** That is the job of the salesperson: to *provide information which will lead to a decision to buy.* In short, it is *persuasion.* Persuading people to think along the same lines that you are thinking. Getting people to *think your way.*

Real Estate Sales Is Really The Most Exciting.

I truly believe that Real Estate sales is really the most exciting sales business of all. You can buy your own products, at reduced rates (your commissions), and build a retirement fund. And Real Estate is one business where you can hit that home run! That's what makes the Real Estate game so exciting. I worked in Real Estate for 6 years before I hit my first home run. I sold 51 subdivided lots in Northridge, CA to Brocke Home Builders and made $151,500. **That** was exciting. Speaking of "the home run," I must tell this "Real Estate" story which happened not too long ago.

The 10 Million Dollar Deal

There is a woman in the Palos Verdes, California area who had had her license, (at this stage of her career, let's call it her "Learner's Permit,") for only about 2 weeks when she met an old acquaintance in the supermarket. Not a friend, mind you. An

"Acquaintance!" During the conversation she mentioned that she had just gotten her real estate license and asked her old acquaintance if she knew of anyone who was looking to buy or sell a house. It turned out that her old acquaintance and husband had been thinking about "trading up" because they had been doing very well lately. So, they started looking at homes in the $2 million price range. They really didn't like those homes very much, so they started looking at more expensive homes. Can you believe it?!! They finally "settled" on a 15,000 square foot new home overlooking the ocean which they purchased for $10 million dollars??!! The property is located on Lower Paseo De La Cresta in Palos Verdes Estates, California and this story can be verified by checking the Multiple Listing Service or tax records for that city. What a mind boggling accomplishment, which realistically, will be difficult to duplicate if she stays in the business another 20 years. But it happened, and I am telling you this for a reason.

Ask *THE* Big Question

It happened, because she asked the question: **"Do you know anyone who is looking to buy or sell a house?"** That is a great way to get business. Whenever you have the opportunity, you should ask that question. Or, a better way, when you are talking to someone ABOUT real estate, ask them if they have any property they are thinking about selling. I could not even guess how many deals I have gotten over the years by simply asking that question. That's how I got the 51 lots. I had been talking with the owner of that property for nearly 3 years about selling his 84 unit apartment building. And during one conversation I just happened to ask, "Oh, by the way Doctor, would you be interested in buying any more large buildings?" He responded by saying that he was looking for another property of between 150 and 200 units, and "By the way, Larry, do you ever sell any land?" "**Well, of course I sell land!!** I sell it everyday!!! What did you have in mind, Doc?????" So, I recommend that you always ask the question. Believe me, business is all around you.

Teaching The *Art* of Selling

Well, I did not decide to write this book to talk about the "home run." Because very few ever get that home run. What I am going to accomplish is to show each and every one who reads through this book, how to get **ONE OR TWO MORE DEALS EACH YEAR**, which I know slip away from every agent because he or she did not do all the things *TRAINED SALESPEOPLE* do when they *"GO TO WORK."* This book is about how to be a *"SALESPERSON,"* not just an agent. I'm going to discuss how you can develop a style of conversation which you can incorporate into your sales presentations which will allow you to uncover objections, and put forth remedies to those objections, in a manner in which you will have your prospects agreeing with you and seeing things *your way*. And at the end of your sale presentation your prospects *will* agree that you are the only *logical* choice to list their property and any further discussions with anyone else would be a waste of *their* valuable time. **This is the art of selling, and it takes practice. Training, if you will.** So, when you finish reading this book remember, you will have to practice and rehearse your presentations so that you feel comfortable with the new material.

Good Salesmanship Is Always A Planned Presentation!

Remember this: no amount of poise, charm, intelligence, or technology can take the place of good salesmanship. Those qualities are good to have, of course, **but, good salesmanship is always:**

1.   **A planned presentation**
2.   **An organized presentation**

3. **A presentation with ready answers to all possible objections.**

Only One Can Be Number ONE

So, let me begin with a question to all who have read this far: In a group of, say 100 sales people, how many in this group can be number one? I'm sure you will agree, the answer is, of course, one. Yes, that's right, one, and only one, can be the number one producer. Now think about that for a few seconds......... Does that mean that all the rest, the other 99, are losers? I don't think so. I don't believe that one person reading this book is the number one producer at his or her firm. Number one never reads books like this one. Mr. or Mrs. Number One does not need me. For what???????? They're number one. What can I tell those people? They have already figured it out and they are too busy to take time to read about what they already know. And you can be sure of this: they aren't going to be telling you. You are their competition!

Efficiency vs. Tricks & Gimmicks

Now for sure, there is nothing wrong with trying to be number one. Nor is there anything wrong with trying to be the best. But reality says that not everyone is the best. However, I am betting that each and every one of you who might be taking the time to read this book, is interested in learning a little something which will make you a little better. A little more *effective* in what you do. Perhaps a ***little gimmick*** which you can learn which will make you just a wee bit more effective in your efforts to earn a living doing what you do. Possibly a ***little trick*** which will enable you to use your hours in a manner to produce more income than what you are now receiving for your efforts. Well, there are a few tricks and gimmicks which I can tell you about, but essentially what I'm going to teach you is how to be more *efficient* in your "Salesmanship." Does the phrase, "Work more effectively," sound familiar?

You can make a good living in the Real Estate business, even if you are not number one. If you look around, you see some people who earn more than you do, and some who earn less. Or perhaps, you are new in Real Estate and *everyone* you see is earning more than you are.

Goals Vs. A Plan

We have all heard of goals. "Write them down!" "Strive to reach them!" Well, what happens when we don't reach them? Are we failures? What then? And how about when we do reach the goals we have jotted down? Do we stop and coast for the rest of the year? Well, goals are important, but you can't reach your goals without a PLAN. *A plan of how to get paid for the work you do.* I love that concept. Getting paid for work we do.

WHAT To Do *WHEN* You Get The Appointment

All Real Estate people have heard of what you must do to get listings. Usually what is taught is that you must "cold call," "door knock," "farm," "join community groups," etc., etc. My information here is not **HOW** to get the "Listing Appointment," because that is a whole other story. I'm going to talk about **WHAT** to do **WHEN** you get the "Listing Appointment," They are hard to get, aren't they? Well, why not have the equipment within you to be sure that you will give the best "Listing" presentation known to mankind? Why not **know** that when you go in for your listing presentation that you are going to be leaving with the signatures?

So, within this guide book I am going to show you ways of presenting your case to your prospects in a prepared and organized manner which will enable you to be sure that when you have finished your presentation, you have done your job. And when, after you have practiced and trained yourselves to do this, you will begin to see your "listing appointments," turn into actual "listings." And this means more money, AND less time wasted. I am sure you will agree with that statement.

When you finish reading, if you have read carefully and thoughtfully, and reflected on what I have written, you *WILL* feel that you have learned something which will change your life in the Real Estate sales business. And perhaps, in your everyday style of conversation!

I am going to relate to you some stories - about myself - about people I have known - about sales presentations. I am hoping that you will be able to identify with some of this information and be able to see ways to improve on your past mistakes.

Your Listing Presentations Are *SALES* Presentations

The first thing which you must do is to start thinking of listing presentations as **"SALES PRESENTATIONS."** Because that is what you are doing when you are trying to get that listing - you are *SELLING* yourself to those property owners. You are a *sales* person.

More Than A Realtor.......

And that reminds me of something. When the idea for this book began percolating around inside my brain, I started looking at all the Realtor business cards that were left at my listings, and those of my office mates. I was looking for the word "*Sales*," or some variation of "*Sales*," on each of those cards. I was **AMAZED** that only about one Realtor business card in 25 had the word "*Sales*" on it describing the attributes of that Realtor! Do you find that as peculiar as I do? I mean, I can find Relocation Specialist, Realtor Associate, Broker Associate, Director, Buyer's Agent, Architect, GRI, MBA, ABR, CRS, BSA, (I made that last one up. Nobody puts BS Artist on their cards). And, I did especially like this one card in particular which I have saved for several years. It read: ***More Than A Realtor***... With three trailing dots after the word Realtor. Come on!!!! What's up with that? Are we embarrassed to be **SALES** people?? Now I look at every business card I get my hands on and look for the word "*Sales*."

The World Needs Realtor Sales People

You all should be proud that you are sales people because you help people buy or sell something they need. Something ***REALLY*** important. They could not do it without you and the proof of that statement is that you exist. If there was no need for Realtor Salespeople, there wouldn't be any! Without you, Real Estate would be a real mess. Can you imagine everyone trying to buy and sell their properties without the help of Realtors? Good grief! It would be **Chaos**! Lawyers would be in ecstasy.

Admit It - We Are Salespeople!

So, I would recommend to you all that if you want to improve yourself in the Real Estate business, the first thing you must do is to **acknowledge** the fact that you are a sales person. Your position in this industry, which you have chosen for yourself, is an individual who must ***SELL*** something in order to prosper. And what a great business it is!

YOUR Clients Are *YOUR* Business

What other business can you think of where you can make so much money and not be required to stay away from home overnight in some motel and away from your family? Where you are not required to spend HOURS on the freeways? Where you must report to an office at a regular time? Where you must play politics in the hopes that you will get a promotion? Where you will worry that you will be out of a job if the company gets sold? Real Estate is great because you can build your own business!! It certainly has it's ups and downs, but **YOUR** clients are *YOUR* BUSINESS!!   If you leave XYZ Real Estate Company, those clients are yours! They don't care about XYZ Real Estate Company, because it was YOU that did the job for them. They are yours for life, if you have a proper program to keep in touch.

II

LISTINGS

Let's talk about listings. Most Real Estate people feel that it is preferable to have listings rather than buyers. When you have listings, you know where your people are. You don't have to worry that they are riding around with some other Realtor because you haven't called them in 3 hours. Or, that they are riding around with you and looking at properties so that they will feel perfectly comfortable when they find that *perfect* property, they can call their Uncle Louie, who just happens to have his Real Estate license hanging in his garage, he can write up the offer. Has anyone ever had those thoughts? How much time do you waste by working with buyers? How about half your life!!!!!!!!!!!!?? But we'll talk about buyers later. Buyers are fun. And making offer presentations is the most fun of all because it is SELLING!

The Three Parts To The Successful Presentation:

Your Appearance

"How Do I Look?"

There are three parts to the successful sales presentation. First of all, you must feel good about yourself and look like you do. If you look happy, you look confident. And happiness rubs off. Some people take this for granted, but you should make an effort to project a happy disposition. **Don't be afraid to ask your friends, "How do I look?"** Let them in on the secret. Try it tomorrow. Or better yet, try it today.

Clothing

And don't be sloppy in your clothing. Remember, if you are meeting someone for the first time, that impression is going to stick with them. You may have built up a nice rapport with your "prospects" on the telephone, but when they *SEE* you, if you don't match up with their image of you, you may lose all credibility. That makes some sense, doesn't it?

A Few Good Pairs Of Shoes.

One thing that I truly believe, from my own experiences and from many opinions I have read, shoes are *REALLY* important. Believe me when I say this, people check out your shoes. When you meet them, they look you right in the eye, but when you are not looking, they will look at your shoes. Think about that. Don't you find yourself doing that when you make your own appraisals of people? I know I do. You can be wearing a $900 suit, but if your shoes look as if you just kicked a brick down the street on the way to the office, you look disheveled. So, spend a little money on a few good pairs of shoes - and keep them polished and in good repair. Repair the heels before you really "have to." It doesn't cost much to put new heels on shoes, and they look bad if the heels are worn down. And you might find that *YOU* feel better when you're wearing a good pair of shoes all nice and shiny. Try it and see if I'm not right about that.

Your Attitude

Next, number two, you must have the **right attitude**. I remember a long time ago, 1973 or 1974, my boss at *PEOPLE MAGAZINE,* Paul Byron, said to me while we were on our way to a meeting with a buyer at a large grocery chain in the Northern Virginia area, "**You can have the best product in the world, but if you don't come to work with the best attitude, you won't get the deal**." Think about that! Does that sound like it makes sense? I have always remembered that comment. He probably had no idea how much impact that comment had on me! It wasn't given in a training class, and he didn't read it out of a manual. He simply shared that idea with me which he had learned over his long life in sales as we were in the car driving over to the meeting. Bingo!

So, if you are having a bad day, either go home and get away from the job, or learn to fake it. As I matured, and I realized my position as a *SALES* professional, I figured out ways to perk myself up if I didn't feel that my attitude was very good that particular day. Knowing how important "**Attitude**" is for my job, I would look around for someone less fortunate than I and just say to myself, "**You think you have problems, Lar? That guy over there has problems. You don't have problems. What you have is an *inconvenience*.**" Can you, the reader, identify with that????? Let's face it. Somebody stood you up for an appointment? Well, I hate when that happens. Don't we all?

Preparation - In Written Form

You selling You

Now, with your *confident look* and *upbeat attitude*, the next part of the equation for the successful presentation is *preparation*. By being prepared, I mean that you should have a written, step by step, plan of how you will make your "SALES" presentation because that's what a listing presentation is. As I mentioned a moment ago, it is *you* selling *yourself*, and your *company*, to these property owners. Remember - the property owner is probably planning to interview 3 Realtors, because that's what he read in the Sunday edition of the Real Estate Section. All your competitors will have the comps, the currently for sale properties, the company history, the personal history, maps, ad copy, etc. etc. Remember - people are impressed by the "sizzle," so make your presentation look fancy.

Only One Realtor Is Getting This Deal

However, remember this too - *only one Realtor is going to get this listing*, so if you are there, that means they still have not decided who it will be. Make your presentation long, and complete! The longer you take, the less likely your prospects will be willing to listen to someone else. So, make sure your presentation is **detailed, interesting**, and maybe a **little humorous**. Project yourself as knowledgeable, professional, and *LIKABLE!!*

Put Yourself In Their Shoes

Good salespeople always remember to imagine themselves in the role of the prospects. "What would I be thinking if I were sitting hear listening to this guy?" So, it's important to be able to view both sides of the presentation. By doing this with your meetings with people, you are more likely to see flaws in your presentation and thereby, be able to modify how you approach the selling scene.

Don't Leave Without The Signatures!!

DETERMINATION

This part is important and may be the one attribute you need to incorporate into your sales disposition which will enable you to get those "almost" deals which have been slipping away from you. After you have developed your presentation in written form, using the information which I am going to give you in this book, together with your own personal touches, you should fortify yourself with **determination** that you are going to make this sale! Your are going to get this listing!! My advice to each and every one of you is this - **don't leave until you have their signatures, or they throw you out of the house!** Because if you leave without the signatures, you have given up your best chance of being paid for your efforts.

You Getting A Call To Come Back = ZERO!

The probability of you getting a call to come back is almost **zero**. So if you must leave without the signatures, at least leave the meeting with the satisfaction that you have ground on them so hard that when you go back to your office there is no way they will be calling you. If you have done a thorough presentation, with all the closes which I am going to give you, these people probably weren't really planning to list their property anyway, and were just interested in finding out what their property was worth. They probably wanted a free appraisal.

I Was Just A Young Pup.

So, doesn't it make sense to have a definite plan when you go in for your presentation? Years ago, when I was a young pup, my sales manager at *Petersen Publishing Company* asked me, "Does a football team go into a game without a game plan?" "Does a pilot leave the airport without a flight plan?" "Does a fighter go into the ring without a fight plan?" Think about that! Of course not. And here is a closer analogy, which I thought up myself: "Does an actor go on stage without first memorizing a script?" *No* to all of the above. So why in the world would a sales person go into a sales presentation without a script?, without a flight plan?, without a game plan?

It's Called: GOOD BUSINESS

Think about this: If you go into a listing presentation with a prepared plan of how you are going to make this presentation, and how you are going to respond to each of the objections that you **know** your prospects are going to use to avoid signing your listing contract, wouldn't you say that you would have an advantage over your competitors? And you will certainly have an advantage over your prospects. I mean, how many times do people sell their homes? You make sales presentations by the dozens. It's not cheating to have an advantage, you know. Ladies and gentlemen, it's called: **GOOD BUSINESS.**

1.   **Preparation**

So, as I mentioned, you must prepare your presentation in a written form. *Don't wing it.* Each listing appointment is an opportunity to make *serious* money, so you want to do your absolute best to get the listing. ***And it's also an opportunity for you to totally waste several hours of your time.*** Think back over the past year and see if you can remember one deal that got away that was almost *there.* Can you remember thinking, "If I had just done this......" Or, "If I had just asked this." What you had just done on that appointment was "prep" those prospects for the next agent in the door. You made it easier for your competition and more painful for yourself when you drove by that property the next morning and saw someone else's *FOR SALE* sign, right? **AND** you wasted time! Probably several hours. If you had prepared your presentation in written form, with the nine modules to signatures which I am going to give you, and had been **ready** for the ten most common objections which I am also going to give you, you probably would have gotten the listing.

Thank You For That *FINE* Presentation!"

You are not in the Real Estate business to give presentations. You are in the business to make money, and I never knew anyone in the Real Estate business who got paid for giving a presentation. Did you ever hear anyone say, "Thank you Mary, for that *fine* presentation - wait just a minute and I'll get your check?" Not hardly. You don't get paid for "Service Calls" in the Real Estate business. Air conditioning repairmen get paid for service calls, but we don't. So, remember:

You must get the signatures!

2.   **The List**

Believe In Yourself!

Make A List

Make a list of all the reasons you can think of why your prospects should list with you. Why are you their best choice? Write these reasons down and put them in order of importance and bring that list with you on every listing appointment. It may be a different list for different appointments, but have the list. And, **believe** the reasons you have listed. This is you!! These are the reasons that make you the best, and *most logical* choice to list their property!!

Who Could Possibly Be A Better Choice??

Think about this: When you go in for that listing presentation, is there really anyone you can think of who would do a better job marketing that property than you???? There really isn't, is there? **So, go in assuming that you are going to get this listing.** Make yourself believe that it is to their advantage to have you as their listing agent. It doesn't matter what reasons you have on your list. One could be that you are the best looking Realtor in town, or that you have the nicest car around, or that you have three cats that you have adopted from the animal shelter and have, thereby, saved those little critters from certain death and therefore, you are a good person. It doesn't matter what the reasons are, just have a list of about ten and while you are giving your presentation, make sure you interject each attribute into the conversation and get them to *agree* with you that that is a good feature and would benefit them. Later I'll explain how important this list will be.

3.   Determine Who's On Title

Another point which is very important when setting up the appointment is determining who, or how many individuals, must agree to sign the listing contract. Usually you can determine this by looking at the property profile.   When discussing the appointment with the prospect, ask if Mary will be there. Will John be there? Will Suzy be there? If all title holders are not going to attend your presentation, you will be doing a "One Legger" presentation. So, you must reschedule.

Avoid The *"One Legger"* Presentation

The 7:00 A.M. Saturday Appointment

I neglected to do this once several years ago and the result was a HUGE amount of wasted time. I had "cultivated" this lead for about 2 years with telephone conversations and mailings. The owner of the property, which was a 14 unit apartment building in Westchester, California lived way down in Southern Orange County in California. Of course, his wife was on title. After many conversations, he finally told me that he had decided to sell the building, but that he was extremely busy and the only time he had available to speak with me was between 6:30 and 7:30 **A.M!** on a Saturday. This meant that I had to be on the road at 5:30 A.M. to make the appointment.

When I arrived at his home, on time, **at 6:30 A.M.,** the first thing he said as he greeted me at the door was that his wife wasn't feeling well and that she was upstairs in bed. **I WAS DEAD IN THE WATER!!**

What do you do in a situation like this? I had spent YEARS working on getting to this moment. I had driven a considerable distance in order to speak with him face to face, and I had spent *hours* putting together my presentation. Color photos, charts, the works. What to do????????????

What I should have done was turn around and walk back to my car and drive down to Denny's for some breakfast. But I did not. Actually, because I knew there was absolutely no way I was going to get this listing without his wife's signatures on the contract, I should have, as politely, but firmly, as possible, informed him that I never gave any information regarding marketing plans, etc., etc. without all parties present. However, I was **weak**! And I proceeded with the warm-up, made my step by step presentation in my planned manner, but when I asked for the signatures, what do you think his response was? You got it. "Gee, it looks good, but I have to have my wife agree with it. You know, I have to live with her." (Oh, wasn't that a nice touch?) "I'll have to get back to you next week."

In this particular case, I don't believe his wife was sick at all. I believe that he had planned the whole thing so that he would not have to make a decision then and there and, in fact, I had been *snookered*. I had walked into a "*One Legger*" presentation which would have been impossible to close and was an example of *TRAP # 1*, of what I call **FOUR TRAPS TO GUARANTEED FAILURE**.

My time had been totally wasted, but it did teach me a lesson. Always try to avoid the "**One Legger**" presentation. Make it known to your prospects that all decision makers must be present in order for you to give them the information they are looking for. By standing up to a prospect requesting a "One Legger" presentation you will save your time. **And** you might get the "respect" that you will need in order to get the listing. What I had given to *this* individual, was just a stack of information which he could use in bargaining with the next Realtor in the door.

Presentations to *"Out-of-Towners"*

Sometimes, of course, if you are dealing with an out of town owner, it would *not* be possible to have everyone present at your presentation. In those instances, you must decide if it is worth your time to prepare a presentation for owners who will not be able to sign the listing during your meeting. If there is no way to group all the owners together, I would recommend that you go ahead with the presentation and try to have someone sign the listing agreement. In a case like this, you probably will have to hope for the best.

III

THE NINE STAGES OF THE SALES PRESENTATION:

Modules

The first stage of any sales presentation is **"Defining the Need of the Prospect."** Of course, in Real Estate listing presentations, we already know the need - the property is to be sold. So, as Real Estate people, we are one step ahead of sales people in other businesses when we prepare our presentations. Therefore, I have omitted that stage from this presentation package because it is a given.

Your listing presentation should be prepared and given in stages, or what I refer to as *"MODULES."* Each module has certain elements, and each element should be discussed before going into the next module. By using the module technique in the presentation, we can control the pace and direction of the presentation *AND* we can obtain certain necessary agreements (closes) from the prospects as we are heading towards getting the signatures. Does that make some sense?? So, in the listing presentation, the first stage, or module, of the sales presentation is:

Module I

Time And Place

Time

Arranging the *time* of the appointment is important. I believe, if you are completely prepared to make the **SALES** presentation and you know that others will be interviewed for the job, it is best to make your appointment at a time when you will be the first one in. If you can schedule your appointment so that you are the first one in, go in confident that you will be leaving with the listing. You are *THE ONE* for this job. **Be sure to have a sign with you in the trunk of your car**. Believe this: you will **never** have a better chance of getting the "Signatures" than this one time when you are there in their home without any distractions. I'm not saying that if you cannot arrange to be the first one in that you should not make the presentation. I'm saying that it is advantageous to be the first one in if you are prepared to be strong. Regardless of what position you are in the lineup, the fact is, if they let you in the door, it means they have not yet made a decision.

Place

Of course, **your meeting place must always be at the home of your prospects.** For example, sometimes you will have an individual who will state that he "conducts all business at the office." Don't fall into this trap, because it is *TRAP # 2*, and is a guarantee for failure. First of all, if you acquiesce to his request for a meeting at his office, the wife probably won't be there and that is his chance to avoid signing your listing and it is *certain death for your presentation*. If you meet at "HIS" office, you have lost any chance of gaining control. Can you see the scenario? He is sitting at *HIS* desk and you are there in a chair, probably lower than his, and you are speaking into his power camp. There might be a telephone ringing right at the point of your close. You are in a subservient position!! You don't have a chance for a close if he has a mind to put you off. *AND*, ...how can you give an estimate on the value of the home if you don't get a chance to look it over, inside and out? If it's a rental property, you still must meet at their home. **Do anything and everything you can think of to avoid meeting at the prospect's office.**

Now, the listing scene.

Larry Hauser

Module II

The Warm-Up

"That Sure Is A Nice Picture Of Elvis"

When you arrive at the home of your prospects, have them show you around. Always pick out one item and compliment them on it. Sometimes this is difficult, but I don't care if it is a picture of Elvis sitting in a café eating a burrito and painted on black velvet hanging over an orange couch, find **something** and admire it. Be careful not to get into too much conversation about it. Remember, we don't want distractions. This is called the **warm-up** and the objective of the **warm-up** is to get them to like you. Without the warm-up, you are just a stranger inside their home. Remember what I said earlier: people will never **BUY** from someone they don't like.

The Glass of Water Ploy.

Another little trick which I have found to be successful in gaining "**warm-up**" is asking for a glass of water. (Never have an alcoholic beverage.) This makes your prospects do something for you. Besides, being thirsty is human. If one of these individuals is a *trained salesperson*, he may recognize this **PLOY** of asking for a drink of water. However, a *trained salesperson*, upon spotting this technique, is likely to gain respect for you and to identify you as one of his/her own. Whatever, ... you want these people to look at you as a regular person, and regular people get thirsty. This early effort when you meet your prospects is necessary to melt away the ice cycles. As I said before, people will "buy" from people they like, so your focus in the warm-up is on getting them to like you. And when they like you, they are more likely to trust you.

Sizing Up Your Prospects

Another reason for the warm-up is the opportunity for you to **size up** your prospects. Who's in charge? Do we have an engineer? Will we be working with an attorney this evening? Are they retired? The experienced salesperson will have a variety of ways to deliver the prepared presentation, depending upon the personalities of the prospects. And remember, as you are sizing up your prospects, they are doing the same with you.

Speed Of Speech

During your warm-up, as you are sizing up your principals, take special notice of how quickly, (or slowly), these people speak. It is important to deliver your presentation, and your entire conversation, in approximately the same speed in which your principals speak. We have all noticed that some people speak in rather slow, deliberate styles, while others speak very quickly. The objective here is to make yourself appear similar to these people to whom you are trying to "**sell**" yourself and your listing program. The exception to this rule is that you do not want to attempt to imitate the extreme. For example: we do not want to attempt to speak in ridiculously slow, or exceedingly high rates of speed. We would probably wind up looking foolish if we did. And of course, we do not want to attempt to imitate a Southern drawl or New York accent, unless we come from those places and it would be natural for us to do that.

(1)
The *"Lay Down"*

So....................., you have to be ready for all types of characters. Of course, the *"Lay Down"* is the best. This is where you don't need a long, drawn out presentation, because these people have already decided that you are going to handle things for them and you are there mainly to do the "paper work." The good thing about the Real Estate business, is that the longer you are in it, the more "lay downs" you get because of your previous business.

(2)
The "*Hard Nose*"

Another type of prospect is what I call the "*Hard Nose.*" You know this guy. He greets you at the door with **"I'm not signing anything tonight."** This guy doesn't know it, but he has just told you, "I want to be sold, *tonight*." If you enjoy sales, like I do, you should be almost ecstatic when you hear this. Now you have an opportunity to do a complete sales presentation with all the objection solving materiel you will have at your disposal after you become a *trained salesperson*. Expect to hear "NO" 6 or 7 times from this guy. And, curiously, you will probably hear very little from his wife. This type of prospect is usually a very domineering individual and his wife should be pitied - but not by you - that's not your job. Your job is to convince this guy that **you are the only logical choice to market his property and further discussion with anyone else would be a waste of his valuable time.**

(3)
The "*Clam*"

Sometimes you run into the individual who doesn't say anything. I call this guy "*The Clam*." Throughout life, these individuals have sat back and listened to people talk while they analyze and evaluate what they are saying. These people are difficult to "read," so it is important to get this individual to participate in the conversation. Therefore, you must make an effort to keep asking him questions, such as,

1) "How long do you want your property to stay on the market?"
2) "Is the *cottage cheese* on the ceilings sealed?"
3) "Do you want people screened before they are brought over to view your home?"
4) "Are you familiar with how the new lock boxes work?"
5) "Did you know that they are planning to put a freeway access ramp right over your home next year?"

Anything! Just make sure you get him to respond to the fact that you exist.

(4)
"I'll List With Whoever Has The Lowest Commission."

Another type is merely a variation of the "Hard Nose." His greeting is: *"I'll list with the one with the least commission."* You have to determine right then, what is this listing worth to you. I have found that when dealing with this type of individual it is important to get him to the table as quickly as possible. A warm-up is not going to provide much benefit, because all he wants to hear is your "number." A statement such as, **"Let me show you what *WE* will do for you and then you tell me what you think *WE'RE* worth,"** is a good question, but it may, or may not, be necessary. I like to say *"We,"* and not *"I"* in this case. This sounds like he will be getting more for his money. It may not fit you, but I like it for myself in this situation. Whatever you do, avoid telling him what your bottom line is as long as possible. He may already have interviewed a few of your competitors and all he needs to know is if he can get it listed for less. What your objective is with this guy is to find out what *his* "number" is.

"What Percentage Do You Want To Pay?"

First, ask him point blank - **"What percentage do you want to pay to get your property sold?"** Make sure you say "percentage." He may have a dollar amount in mind, but start out with "percentage." He may say he wants to pay X number of dollars, but you should go back with something like, "We always work in percentages in this business, Mr. Jones, so let's talk in percentages." Ask him some questions, such as, "How many other Realtors have you interviewed so far?" **Keep asking him what his number is until he tells you**. Whatever it is, briefly go over what is required in marketing his property. Make it as brief as possible, because he really doesn't care. **However, with each item you discuss in your brief presentation, ask him if he thinks it is necessary in getting his property sold.** For example, "We normally run picture ads in the local paper with listings like yours. Do you think we need to do this with your property??" This is important, because many times these individuals have *no* idea what it takes to sell a property and have determined that it really should not cost him anymore than say, $2,500 for the whole thing.

Be Abrupt - Pin Him Down

After you have gone over, as I said, very briefly, your marketing plan for properties like his, ask him this question: **"If I agree on a brokerage fee with you here at this table, will you sign this listing agreement before I walk out of here?"** If the answer is "No," ask him why not. Try to pin him down. Tell him that you are not going to cut your fees to the bone, and then have another Realtor come in and do it for $50 less.

Get Him To Commit - Right Now

Ask him, **"You wouldn't do that if you were me, would you?"** This type of individual respects a person who is strong and does not appear intimidated by his abruptness. If you can get him to agree to sign your listing if you can agree on a commission amount, start negotiating your fees. If you can meet his number, take the listing. If not, it does not necessarily mean that you have done a poor sales job. You have saved yourself time and trouble and you can leave this guy to abuse one of your competitors. When you are driving down the road after leaving this guy, don't feel as if you have failed. You have not undersold yourself and you have gained some experience for the next time. If you have handled this guy properly, you have not revealed your bottom line because he failed to commit to you for the listing. Be proud of yourself for not caving in to this domineering individual. And be happy that your competitor is going to have to deal with him for a minimal fee. You might even reward yourself with a little chuckle.

Module III

Pick Your Spot

Avoid TRAP #3

When you feel that you have "warmed up" the prospects, which should never be longer than 15 or 20 minutes at most, you must guide the "meeting" to the kitchen table. **Never, ever, allow them to guide you anywhere but to the table, because if you do, you will fall into TRAP #3**. If the kitchen table is unavailable for some reason, get to the dining room table. All business is done at the kitchen table or the dining room table. Believe me when I tell you this, your chances of getting a signature, which is really the **ONLY** reason you are there, is almost 100% NIL if you do not conduct your presentation at the table.

Avoid The "Home" Office.

Sometimes, when you arrive at the HOME of the prospect they will attempt to have this "meeting" in an office which they have set up at home. This is more and more common today where many people have "home offices." Once again, do your best to get to the kitchen or dining table. These people might think that it is best to conduct "business" in their "office," but we know that we are placed in a subservient position even in a "home office." Besides, many times there will be a separate "business" line in the home office, and if that phone rings during our presentation, it will detract from the continuity of the presentation. Remember, we do not want distractions during our *controlled* presentation.

Allow me to digress for a moment here and tell you a little story about how I was confronted with a difficult situation several years ago.

Jimmy 'n Sugar

At the time, I was selling **Long Term Health Care Insurance** for **GE Capital** and I had an appointment with an older couple who owned a home in the La Canada-Flintridge area north of Los Angeles. I arrived at their home at about 7:00 P.M. When I rang the door bell, two dogs came running out from the back yard barking like crazy. They were not attacking me, but they were making quite a racket. When the prospects let me in, the dogs came in too, still barking like wild animals. The owners finally quieted them down and I attempted the "warm-up."

What I Had For That Evening Was A Pair Of "Collectors"

Now, these people were "collectors." I'm sure that those of you who have been in this business a while know what I mean when I say, "collectors." Collectors are people who have a hard time throwing anything away. They are usually older people and their homes are, let's say, cluttered. Well, these folks, and I still remember their names, Jimmy and Shirley, who incidentally, was addressed as "Sugar" by Jimmy with his Texas accent, also had a bird collection. Actually, it was a little business they had and there were bird cages of all different sizes in every room all throughout the house. The back yard patio was one huge bird cage. There were all kinds of different birds which they told me they raised and sold to pet shops and individuals.

The Kitchen or Dining Table Were "Not Available."

Back inside the house, I continued with the warm up, trying to find something about this mess which I had been walking through to compliment them on. I finally settled on the unusual rock fire place they had which went straight to the top of the cathedral ceiling. While we had been walking through the house

29

Larry Hauser

I noticed that there were several birds loose inside, flying around at will. I also had "eyeballed" both the kitchen table and dining room table and noticed that they were both stacked about 4 feet high with "stuff." There wasn't a square inch of space at either table and not a prayer of getting either cleaned off so that we could sit down and have the presentation. I should have left right then, and gone to the driving range to hit some golf balls until dark. But, because I was **THERE**, I decided to do the presentation.

There Were Just Too Many Distractions.

The only place to sit was on the couch, which had newspapers piled up on the floor to the tops of the arms on both sides. "Sugar" sat in a big easy chair across from the sofa, and I sat in the middle of the sofa with Jimmy on my right. As we discussed the need for my product, they related to me their reason for their interest in this type of insurance. Without my getting into details here, they were solid prospects for this type of product because of a situation with Jimmy's parents and how their entire estate had evaporated because of health care costs. So, this conversation is what I would call, as serious as a heart attack. But, as I was looking across at "Sugar," one of the birds had landed on her head and was bobbing up and down. She was sitting there as serious as could be, and I was looking at this bird doing a dance on top of her head. Can you picture this ridiculous scene?   .... **Concentration on the primary subject was difficult!** The next distraction came from the dogs. Every time someone walked past the front gate, they would run over, jump up on the couch between Jimmy and me, and bark like crazy through the picture window behind the couch. Finally, Jimmy got them to calm down, but the big one, a German Shepard, had taken a liking to me. He started to lean against me as I was giving this very serious presentation. This was a big dog, and every time he leaned on me, I moved over a little bit, trying to ignore the distraction and continue with my presentation. And every time I moved over, Jimmy would yell at the dog to quit bothering me. It was very difficult to present my information with these distractions. Finally, the dog had pushed me completely to the end of the couch and I moved up to the arm of the couch. That's when Jimmy jumped up and yelled, **"That's it!! Sugar, get me the rope!"** So, Sugar got up, went into the other room and came back with this rope that was thick enough to tie up the Titanic, and threw it on the floor in the middle of the living room. Believe me when I say it, the presentation was getting away from me! Jimmy wrapped a noose around the dog's neck and dragged him out the front door and came back inside.

Sometimes You Must Concede Defeat In Your Presentation.

With the dog outside, I attempted to get the presentation back on track. Jimmy on one side of me, and Sugar in front, with the dancing bird on her head, all attention and ready to listen to me about this very important matter. Almost immediately, I heard the dog scratching and whining at the front door. I tried to ignore it and continued with my step by step presentation; Jimmy 'n Sugar agreeing with every precept I put forth. After less than 5 minutes the noise at the front door had gotten so loud that it sounded like a grizzly bear trying to get inside. Impossible! That's when Sugar interrupted me and yelled, "Will you lookee there - he's turnin' the handle - he's turnin' the handle!" That was it! That meeting was over. This case was **CLOSED!!** I shook my head, closed my presentation manual, thanked them for their time, and headed towards the door. They apologized and asked me if I could come back tomorrow, but I declined. I gave them my card and told them if they wanted to come to my office in Newport Beach without the dogs I would be glad to give them the rest of the information. Of course, I never heard from them and they probably used my card to pick corn out of their teeth after I drove away.

Larry Hauser

You Must Control The Presentation Or You Will Fail.

The moral of this story is this: If you can't give a presentation on the kitchen (or dining) table, **forget it!!!** Go home. Don't be weak. Do not compromise yourself. Do not allow the prospect to control the meeting, because if you do - you have lost. You are a professional and you will have the prospects' respect. You may not get the contract later, but you won't get it without that sit down at the table. You will be wasting your time and merely helping your competition.

Module IV

Positioning Your Prospects

After determining which table you will use for your presentation, you must position your prospects with two things in mind:

1) Make certain that if there is more than one prospect, and usually you will have a couple, that **both are situated in front of you**. This is easy if the table is round, but many tables are oblong or rectangular and it is possible for you to wind up in the middle with the husband on one side and the wife on the other. This positioning is very important, because as you are giving your presentation it is easy for you to appear to be speaking more to one than the other. Also, and this has happened to me, one of the prospects could be making signs to the other when you are looking the other way. Such as pointing to their watch, or rolling their eyes. You avoid this by having them both in front of you.

2) The second point to consider when positioning your prospects is to make sure you **do not sit closest to the member who is the same gender that you are.** Very often, unbeknownst to the salesperson, the man may feel a bit jealous of the salesman, and vice versa with a saleswoman. This happens more often than most people realize, so it is just a precautionary measure which the *trained salesperson* can take when positioning the prospects. Remember, you are putting forth your best face with your presentation and who knows what is going on in their relationship. You are there for business, so you don't want anything to get in the way of your goal: *a signed listing agreement.*

Was He Deaf or Jealous?

I remember a time when I was giving this fine presentation to an older couple whom I had determined was selling their large home and moving to a smaller, one level home. Mrs. Jones was at one end of the table, and Mr. Jones was at the other. I was in the middle, between the two, and thinking I was giving a fine presentation of myself and my company. They were both agreeing with all my statements. After a while, I had switched my efforts mostly to Mrs. Jones. She was being more responsive, so I had virtually stopped even looking in *Mr. Jones'* direction.

"Just Leave It And I'll Have My Lawyer Look It Over."

At the completion of the presentation I started to fill out the listing form and he asked me what I was doing. After I told him that I was beginning the "paper work" he said that I should leave it and he would have his "lawyer" look it over and then get back to me. **"WHA-A-A-AT??"** Need I say it? **A total and complete waste of time**. I had gotten her to agree to everything I had projected, but he had totally clammed up. After several closes, I realized that this guy *had not even heard a word that I had said during the previous hour*! He was very hard of hearing and only "heard" when he could read someone's lips, that is, when they were speaking directly at him. I doubt if a jealousy factor had played a part in this fiasco because the two were easily 25 years older than I was. But the result was: NO SALE. A complete waste of many hours of my time because I had not followed the known precept of placing all prospects in front of me!

"Split Prospects" = *"No Sale."*

However, if I had taken the trouble to arrange my prospects properly at that table, I would have noticed that he had had a hearing impairment, and I would have adapted my presentation for his behalf. The results would have been quite different. But because I had not followed this simple rule of getting *"all prospects in front"* I had lost my chance of a successful listing presentation and I went home empty handed. I never allowed that to happen to me again.

I'm telling you this because it is an easy problem to avoid, but it is just as easy to not notice - until it is too late. Once you are seated, it is difficult to rearrange your position at the table.

Module V

Establish Urgency

Before making the actual time for the appointment, you should have determined *the reason for selling*. A quick question in the initial conversation, either on the phone or at an open house, is usually easily answered by the prospect. It is a non-threatening question, and they are usually quite willing to answer it truthfully. It's a good conversation question. And it is very important because it determines the **level of urgency for the sale**. With this information, it is possible that you might modify your usual marketing plan and presentation to fit this need.

"Prospect Cultivation" is Necessary In Any Sales Business.

For example: if you determine that the prospects are not really ready to sell their property, you should ask yourself if you have the time to spend with people who aren't really ready to sell. There is nothing wrong with spending time with prospects who really have not made up their minds yet about selling. Very simply, you may find value in "cultivating" these prospects, because "cultivation" is usually how seasoned agents maintain a steady flow of business over the years. In fact, it is necessary for long term success in any sales business.

Avoid "TRAP #4"

So, if you determine through your initial questioning that there is no immediate urgency to sell, be careful about giving away too much information which should be saved for your presentation. **Above all, avoid any conversation about commissions at this point.** This is **TRAP # 4 to guaranteed failure**, and I will get to it in a minute. Just remember, in a prepared sales presentation, there is a specific spot to speak about commissions, or what you can refer to as **"Brokerage Fees,"** if you like.

Laying Out The Listing Agreement With The Cost Sheet

Question #1: The "NEED"

If you have made the appointment because you have determined that your prospects have decided to sell now, you should *reconfirm* their reason for selling when you sit down at the table. I call this Question #1 and should always be used as the first question when getting down to business. It is the classic *"NEED"* question. **"Well, Mr. & Mrs. Jones, you told me on the phone that you have decided to sell your home because you have gotten a transfer."** (Or, whatever.) This will start the procedure with your principals agreeing to your question.

An Absolute *MUST*!

While you are all settling down at the table and they are answering your question about *need*, you should be busy laying out all your material on the table. All of your comps, maps, ad copy, etc. goes on the table. And along with this material, **you *must* lay out the *listing contract* in full sight of your prospects**, and a *cost sheet*. Don't place this material directly in front of them, but **that contract and cost sheet should be out in plain sight**. It's very important.

Your presentation has just begun with you asking the first question and getting them to agree with you. An important direction. **"Yes," is what you want to hear**, but ultimately agreement with what you say, because at the end of your presentation, you want them to take your pen and sign their names to where you are pointing on the contract you have just completed. Right?

Question #2: The "PROBE"

Now, after you all have settled down at the table and are comfortable, **AND** you have asked them question # 1 regarding why they are selling their property, it is time to ask Question #2. It usually goes something like this: **"Well, Mr. & Mrs. Jones, you have obviously made a very important decision in deciding to sell your home. And equally important in the process is deciding who is going to do the job for you. So, it's usually at this point that I ask people 'What are you looking for in the person you chose to do this very important job for you?'"** This question is the classic *"PROBE"* question. By asking them this question, **BEFORE** you begin your actual presentation, you can obtain information which you can use at the end of your presentation if they put off signing the listing agreement.

It is also a chance for your people to talk about things which are of interest to them. Remember, people like to talk about themselves - *it's only natural*. If you can get your prospects to talk a bit about what they perceive to be important regarding the sale of their property, they will become more relaxed and comfortable with you sitting across the table from them.

Jot Down Any Requirement They Give You On Your Note Pad.

Some people will give you a very detailed list of what they are looking for in a Realtor, others will try to avoid answering specifically. Regardless of the type of individuals you are working with, jot down any information they give you on the note pad which you have laid out with your other materiel. When you get into the delivery of your presentation, make sure that you remind them of how certain parts of your "Plan" coincide with their requirements of *"The Perfect Realtor"* for them.

Becoming *FAB*-ulous

Sometimes, after you have inspected the home, or have sat down with your prospects and determined that they might be better off to wait one or two weeks before putting the home on the market, there is the temptation to reschedule the actual "listing" appointment to a later date. My recommendation is that you try for the signatures regardless. Even if you have a very close relationship with these people, there is too much opportunity for them to be scooped up by another, more aggressive, Realtor.

How About A Paint Job?

For example, if it is decided that it would be better to have the home painted before putting it on the market, suggest to them that, by listing the property with you now, you might be able to locate a buyer, quietly through your office alone, who would be more interested in doing the painting himself. If you could do that for them, they would not have to bother about putting out some cash, or scheduling painters to come to their home. You have just *FAB*ed them! That's a **FEATURE** (office exclusive), **ADVANTAGE** (you might be able to get a buyer right away), and **BENEFIT** (they would not have to spend cash and bother with painters).

Always Try For The Signatures.

Remember what I said earlier, if you are **THERE**, it may be the best chance you ever have of getting the signatures. You can tell them that you will hold the listing off the MLS until they have the painting done, (or the driveway repaired, or the sod put in the front yard, etc.), and by the way, if you can't locate a buyer in a few weeks who is interested in doing his own painting, could you perhaps help them arrange for a painter to do the job? Or, "You know, there is a fellow in my office who has a concrete guy he has worked with for quite a while. I understand that he has done some really great jobs with driveways. Would you like me to have him come over here and give you an estimate?" **Leave with the signatures, if possible!!** And, of course, always carry the waiver which allows you to keep the listing off the MLS for a period of time. That would be signed AFTER the listing contract. **"Oh, by the way, just okay this waiver for me would you?"**

Thanks For All Your Help

I remember the story this fellow in my office told me about how he had worked with a guy for 3 months helping him get his house "fixed" up so that he could list it. He had been over there twenty times with painters, carpenters, landscapers, masons, etc. while the prospect had been "at work." He had acted virtually as the General Contractor. One day, when all the work was just about completed, he drove past the house and saw a Re/Max sign on the front lawn. He told me he almost had a stroke!! He couldn't believe it!!! He tried, unsuccessfully of course, to contact the guy by phone for 2 days before finally going right to his house. This bum told him that the Re/Max agent had come to his door to compliment him on what a beautiful job he was doing on his house and that she had a buyer who had asked her to contact the owner. Need I continue?? My friend got nothing for all his efforts. Well, not really nothing!!! He did get a "lesson." And the Re/Max agent? I think she must have been at one of my classes. So remember:

Get the signatures!!!!

Module VI

Laying Out The Marketing Plan

Naturally, your prospects are interested in what you have done recently, but remember this: **People only care about one thing - themselves**. They only care about their own property. Therefore, you must make them feel that what you are displaying in front of them is the *unique marketing plan for their property*. Most of us have access to a digital camera now and I'm sure we all have access to computers. So, it is a great idea to drive past the property before your appointment time and take a few digital shots, return to the office, and load the best front shot onto a flier format which you should have ready on your hard disc. Tailor this flier for the subject property, leave the price window with just a dollar sign, print out a few color samples (one for each of your prospects), and include this in your presentation. This is impressive to clients, even though all your competitors are probably doing the same thing. However, if you are on schedule here, yours will be the first they see, and hopefully, the last because they are going to sign before you leave, right?

Determine Property Price Now

During this section of your planned presentation, you will have the opportunity to show them your Comparative Market Analysis. They should be eager to see this, to reconfirm their own thoughts as to the value of their property. After reviewing the comps and currently for sale properties, you might ask them what price they think should be asked for their property. Usually, their thoughts about price will be pretty close to yours, but if it's not, it's no big deal. Just get them to agree on a price - hopefully not too much higher than what you think it should be. We know that we have all been wrong in pricing, so get them to agree that the "market will tell" what the real price will be. **Just get a price. It is a necessary building block for your close.**

How To Avoid Objections Before They Become Objections.

Also, during this section of your sales presentation, the *Laying Out of The Marketing Plan,* you will have an opportunity to address a number of objections *before* they become objections. This is very crafty on your part, and a benefit of your planned presentation. Because by addressing these POSSIBLE objections early, you can thereby avoid them being obstacles at the end of your presentation! Remember earlier that I told you that you must have a *list of reasons* why these prospects should select you to list their property? This is where your "LIST" is employed.

A Few Examples

For example: "Mr. & Mrs. Jones, I have found that most Real Estate agents are women and that means that most times the offers that come in are presented by women representing their buyers. Now, over the years I have discovered that if I am sitting across the table from a woman Realtor, it is just a teeny bit easier in the negotiating process when we are trying to put a transaction together. Can you picture that scenario at your table when we get an offer?" **WAIT FOR AN ANSWER!** It is important that you get them to agree with you on this matter. And isn't it a neat little "assumptive" close?

By bringing up this *feature* to your prospects early on, and pointing out how this could be an *advantage* to them in the negotiating process, and could ultimately *benefit* them in the end, you have overcome a possible hidden objection which they might have regarding preferences as to what gender their listing agent should be. Of course, if you are a woman Realtor, reverse the benefit. Whatever gender you are, it is definitely the best gender to be in the Real Estate business, right?

The Age "Benefit"

Another example might be a discussion regarding your age: "Mr. & Mrs. Jones, I know that I look young, but the fact is, this has really helped me in this business. I just don't get tired out like some of the older people I see in my business. Don't you think it is a good idea to have someone representing you that has a lot of energy?" **Could they possibly say "NO?"**

Or, you could reverse that if you are like me - older with plenty of gray hair. "Mr. & Mrs. Jones, I have been doing this business for a long time and I can't even begin to tell you how much better I am at it than I was 10 or 15 years ago. Granted, most Real Estate agents will do a good job in marketing and getting your home sold, but if there are some surprises near the end of the escrow period and you don't have that experienced agent working for you, I'm sure you'll agree that it's too late to make a change at that time. I guess it's my experience of doing so many transactions over the years, because I find that when my deals are done, there are no complaints from either buyers or sellers. All the details have been addressed and agreed upon by all parties. **As a matter of fact, let me show you a few testimonials I have from some clients who have worked with me."** Here is your chance to bring out those testimonials I mentioned earlier."

Can you see the benefit of having this LIST with you? Whatever assets you have listed about yourself on your LIST, this is an opportunity to bring out a few and *FAB* the Jones'. Call it a *cheat sheet* if you like, but with proper use you can avoid several objections which Mr. & Mrs. Jones might use at the end of your presentation when you slide your pen over to them.

Module VII

Setting The Stage For The Order

or

The Set-Up

During your conversation at the table about what you are going to do for them, always attempt to appear in the affirmative. That is, speak as if it is assumed they are going to sign the listing agreement. For example:

"When we get our first offer……….": Or,

"Will you be here tomorrow when I come back to take the interior pictures?"

By asking all these questions during your presentation, you are projecting a picture to them of *you* as their listing agent.

The Escrow Question: A Must!

"How long of an escrow period (or "settlement" period—depending upon what part of the country you're from) do you people want after we have accepted the offer?" This question is very important, and *must* be asked during the set up. Later, you will see why.

"We use ………Escrow Company. Have you heard of them?"

Be conversational, but do not get side tracked. Be focused! Remember that each question you ask is for a *specific* purpose. Each question is a building block to your presentation, which if followed precisely according to your "Plan," will guide you to the successful close. At the end, after you have gotten them to agree with everything you have projected, there is really nothing *logical* for them to do but to sign the listing contract. Right??

The Use of Open Ended Questions

Everyone should know what material content to have for the presentation, so I'm not going to get into that. The important thing is for you to find out what they want from the real estate person whom they chose to list their property for sale. You determine this by **ASKING** them. As we discussed before, while we were laying out the Listing Agreement and Cost Sheet, we used the **"PROBE"** question. This is the proverbial **OPEN ENDED** question. The open ended question allows them to elaborate a little bit, and more importantly, do some talking. Very often it is too easy to slip into a monologue when making your presentation. We know what we want to say. We have it down. We can get real blabby, because sales people are just naturally blabby. But, when we talk too much, we really cannot determine if our prospects are really listening to what we are saying unless we get them into the conversation. So, ask questions. **"What do you expect from the Realtor you chose to market your property."** Or, **"Where do you think the most effective advertising would be for your home."** Get them involved.

The Use of Closed Ended Questions

Or, a closed ended question, **"Do you think this is a good spot in this magazine to have a picture of your home?"** Closed ended questions are handy tools, if used properly. By having your prospects in front of you, when you ask that yes, or no type of question, YOU can control the response. Try asking, **"Don't you like this flier that we use for our listings?"** *while at the same time nodding your head in the affirmative*. What are they going to say? "No, that's a really bad flier." They will see you nodding your head and of course, they will agree. Or, **"If we price your property too high in relation to the market, it could sit a long time. You don't want this to go on too long, do you?"** At the same time, shaking your head in the negative.

Get them to do some head nodding if possible. It will keep them awake and they will be thinking your way.

Other Closed Ended questions which I have found to be valuable in a sales presentation are:

(1)   **"That's sounds reasonable, doesn't it?"** Or,
(2)   **"That makes sense, doesn't it?"**
(3)   Or, one of my real favorites, **"You would agree with that, wouldn't you?"**
(4)   And of course, **"That's a good idea, right??**

After you have detailed what the marketing plan should be, you should have developed an easy conversation between you and your prospects. So, then it is on to the next step.

Explain Your Job.

Make sure that you mention to them that it is your job to **"produce offers from the market place."** Reconfirm your commitment to the MLS: **"That's how you determine the *REAL* market value of your property - by giving it the full exposure to all the buyers in the market place."**

You Don't Set The Price.

Emphasize to these people that YOU do not set the price. All you can do is help them with their **ASKING PRICE**. Whatever offers you can *generate* from the market place are determined by forces outside of your control: i.e. other agents working independently with their buyers. By doing this, you have set yourself up to be NEUTRAL when an offer comes in that is not perfect in every way.

Watch Out For "*Nasty*" Buyers' Agents.

Does this sound strange to some of you "*Seasoned*" agents? I know that it sounded rather strange to me when I was newer in the business because I thought it was my job to "protect" my sellers from nasty buyers' agents who brought in low offers. Who knows how many "DEALS" I talked myself out of until an old salt of a Realtor, Dick Joyce of Moore & Associates in Torrance, California, told me the value of the ability to know how and when to **SHUT UP**.

Dick told me something one day, after I had just "counseled" my sellers regarding a low offer which we had just received. I mentioned to Dick that my sellers and I had just been presented an offer in the old fashioned way, i.e. face to face, from some very nice Realtor from another company. I was complaining to him that the offer was low and I had shown the comps to the other agent and had recommended to the sellers that *WE* counter back at a price very close to our asking price - based of course, on the comps. The other agent thanked us, and left with the counter offer and we never heard from her again. *Gone like a puff of smoke*! Dick, in his patented sarcastic way, had congratulated me for just having talked myself, and my sellers, out of a deal.

I Had The Ability To KNOW The Market Value!

We had not had an offer on that property for more than 4 weeks of market time!! Does that give a signal to anyone reading this book? Because I was so in *LOVE WITH MYSELF* and my ability to *KNOW* what the market value of that home was, I blew it for myself, and the sellers.

The Market Price For Any Property Is What Is On The Table!

I have learned, from experience, that I do not know what the exact market value is of any property. **As a sellers' agent, my duty is to get the deal done!** Unless there is another offer being held by another buyer's agent sitting in the car out front, the market price for that property may very well be what is lying on the table in front of you.

Make The Sellers Decide.

The sellers must make the decision as to whether to accept, reject, or counter the offer and that scenario should be suggested to your prospects when you are making your presentation. How foolish we look when we recommend countering back at such and such a price, and the buyer disappears. And, when no other offers come in during the remainder of your listing period, how difficult it is to extend that listing period when the sellers have been sitting around saying, "You know, if we hadn't listened to Charlie, *OUR REAL ESTATE EXPERT*, we would be out of here by now.

Prepare Your Sellers For Low Offers.

So, be sure to interject into your presentation the possibility of low offers coming in on their property. Everyone has the right to try for the highest price for their homes and investment properties, but they must realize that the market may not produce the desired selling price. Put the weight on their shoulders and let them know that you will be there to answer their questions, of course, but that it is their property, and therefore, their decision as to what price to accept.

The Concept Of *"Let The Sellers Decide."*

This concept, *"Let your sellers decide*," will help you over the long run. Be careful not to talk yourself out of deals.

Module VIII

The Commission

One of the last things to come up, in an orderly presentation, is the commission. Of course, we know by the rules of the DRE, we have to be careful here. So, I am going to state right here: **I am not professing that we should SET our commissions. Nor shall we collude to SET our commissions.** All I am saying is: **Do not sell yourself short.** I am always amazed when I am approached by a salesman, or sales woman, and the first thing they say is, "The regular price for this is $4,000, but I can sell it to you for $3,200." Where do you go from there????? Answer: You go lower!!! I am immediately tipped off that I am dealing not with a salesperson, but more likely a sales rep! Easy "pickin's."

The commission question is usually phrased, **"How much do you charge?"** Many times the prospects will ask you this question early on. As I mentioned earlier, avoid answering this question until **YOU** are ready to answer it. Do not answer this question directly until you arrive at that *specific part* in your sales presentation. Your response should be something like, **"That's important, and I'll get to it in a minute, but let me show you what we do with our advertising (or, whatever) first."**

All Realtors Are Over Paid - It's A Fact!

Now, it is a well known fact that Realtors are all over paid and that they get 6% about 60 days after they have a few papers signed and then go down to escrow to pick up the check and from there go directly to the airport, usually in a limo, for a vacation. Remember this: no matter how much you have told them about what it takes to get their property sold, they have heard from **SOMEONE**, that they can get it done for less than the full commission. Many times, a **LOT** less. So, you have to set a limit on how low you will go in your commission arrangement. You certainly don't want to walk away from a good, marketable listing for a few commission dollars, but don't go in with, "Yeah, I do it for such and such." Because then your prospects will think they can get it for less. That is a fact, and it is the most common example I can think of where a group of people give away the store. **Always TRY for as much commission as you think you are worth**. (Here is a little math exercise for you: figure out how much more you would have made last year if all your commissions had been based on a full commission listing agreement. After all the work you must do to run a transaction through to completion, don't you think you are worth the full commission?)

Laying Your Hands on the Listing Contract

A Crafty Strategy

After you have presented your case in the correct order, go back to his question, "How much do you charge?" **"Well, it says right here, real estate commissions are negotiable."** Point out the bold type regarding commissions.

This is a critical point in your planned presentation because it allows you a chance to lay your hands on the listing document and put it in front of them. I want to emphasize "Critical Point!" Because it is already on the table, you don't have to do anything scary, such as reach into your brief case for a contract!! WOW!! Is that scary to the prospects. Point out the bold type in the contract regarding commissions. "Our usual fee is such & such, which is split 50 - 50 with the agent who drives the buyers around for 3 months and finally gets them to write an offer to purchase your property." "And then, of course, a portion of my side goes to my broker who pays all the bills to keep our office open, as well as the advertising. It's expensive to be in business today, ya know. Do you realize that our office has an advertising budget of $10,000 per month? (Or, whatever.) So, we usually charge such & such."

Don't ask: "Is.......% okay with you?" *Of course, this answer will be no.* This is the hardest question to get answered in the affirmative, but it is the actual first step in actually beginning to fill out the listing contract. At this time, the opportunity has arrived for you to produce your *"ESTIMATE OF COSTS"* sheet. **You must have this sheet right at hand.**

"Mr. & Mrs. Jones, let's try to figure out what your net proceeds will be if we accept an offer at $XXXXXXX." Once again, use the phrase with "we" in it. Just start filling in the numbers. Be assumptive!

"By the way, Mr. & Mrs. Jones, what is the approximate balance on your mortgage loan?" (Get them involved in the process!!)

Do you know whether or not there is a pre-payment fee on your loan? (This figure could be substantial and could effect the entire transaction. If there is a pre-pay, bring it out into the open.)

The Importance of the Cost Sheet

Another Crafty Move

Very diligently fill in all the expenses, at the same time chatting with them and pointing out how you are arriving at the charges, i.e. escrow fees, transfer fees, title fees. Be knowledgeable. **"Oh, by the way, I can get you a nice discount on your title policy. I have a very good relationship with ...."** *Show them the rate schedule.* You should have a close relationship with one title insurance rep who can arrange for the "short term" rate. This is your chance to demonstrate your value to them. If you have trouble with some items, such as prorations, which I always felt uncomfortable fiddling around with, just say, **"this is done through escrow,"** and mark it that way on your sheet. On your cost sheet try to have as many different charges as you can think of. (You can design your own cost sheet on the Microsoft Excel program and have their property address printed out. Once again, you have *personalized* your presentation for *their* property - the only one they really care about.) Don't bunch up the costs. Let them begin to get the picture that it is very involved getting a home sold and **closed!** When you come to the charge for the "Home Buyers' Protection Policy" you can throw this in as part of your special program if you would like. Make this seem like a big deal. **Go over the importance of a "Home Buyers' Protection Plan" for them, as well as for the buyers, when you arrive at this entry on your cost sheet.** So, by you providing this policy for them, you are making your program appear very complete! And a good deal! Remember - everybody likes to get a deal!

Don't Speak It!

After you have completed the costs, with the commission amount you want to charge for this listing, and have determined an *APPROXIMATE* net figure, show it to them and ask them what they think. *If you detect some negative vibes, go to the commission.* If you feel that they are balking at the full commission, don't cave in yet. It is easy for you to give in at this point, but do not forget what I mentioned earlier about persistence. Go over what you are going to do, what it takes for another agent to get a buyer, and what a presence your company has in the area. Then ask again. **"Is this number bothering you, Mr. Jones?"**

(Point to it on the sheet, **DON'T SPEAK IT!!**) If the answer is still "No" to your commission fee, ask him what he wants to pay. *Get him to give you HIS number*. This will allow you to determine if he has been contaminated by others telling him what his commission should be. Don't become argumentative. Be reasonable. Find out what his number is and determine if you can meet it.

Do Some "Horse Trading"

If it is too low, do some horse trading. "We could do away with open houses and not put advertising in these expensive magazines, if you want that percentage. But, we could do the entire marketing package which I have shown you for, say, ____%." Wait for an answer. **Don't speak**. The next sound should come from the other side of the table. Still too high? Don't walk away! "Okay, Mr. Jones, you are a very difficult negotiator, but I believe that your property is very marketable at the price we have agreed upon, so I will do it at your price and I know I'll have a good time working with you for the next several months." "I really enjoy this business, because I can, more or less, chose who I want to work for. Not a bad business, don't you agree?"

Fill In The Commission Amount

At this point, take the listing agreement, which should be right next to you on the table, and fill in the commission amount. It is *extremely important* to get this commission amount entered into the listing contract at this point, because this is the first time you will have actually written something on this contract!!! Do this quickly and then immediately go to the paragraph in the contract where it says *Additional Terms*, and put in **"Escrow period to be—days, unless otherwise stated."** We, as **TRAINED** Real Estate **SALES** agents know that it is entirely unnecessary in the context of marketing this property to write in this term of sale in the contract. However, in our **SELLING** strategy, it is an opportunity to physically place another item in this scary looking contract. Remember, it is important to complete both of these entries *quickly*, so that you can get back to the discussion leading to obtaining the signatures for the listing.

Your next question, after you have completed the commission portion should be something like, **"We can do the**

listing for 90 days, but I really prefer 180 days because it takes a little while to get all the advertising lined up. Is 180 days okay with you?" (Or whatever listing periods you feel comfortable with.) If they say "No," ask them what listing period they had in mind. Sometimes you will even have to negotiate with your principals on the listing period. The important thing is to get them to say "Yes." If they say "Yes," to this question, you have probably successfully closed this deal. So, complete the part on the listing agreement which specifies the listing period and continue on through the entire contract. Congratulations. You have succeeded in obtaining the listing.

However..........................sometimes it doesn't go quite this well. We all know that, don't we?

Module IX

Closing and Overcoming Objections

EXPECT THEM TO SAY "NO"

You Are Not A Friend

The final "Module" of the sales presentation, if you have not gotten the prospects to sign your listing agreement by this time, is "**Closing and Overcoming Objections.**"

Now the real "selling" begins. It's true that you have made an effort to become "*friends*" with these people in your Warm-Up and throughout your presentation to this point. But remember this: if you don't get this listing, **there is no friendship**. You will be forgotten in 24 hours, **or 24 seconds**! *AND* - they will be making friends with your competitors. So, what you must do, as the sales professional, is to *appear* to be their "*friend*," but keep in mind that they are actually your "*opponent*." They have something you want, so you **MUST** keep focused on getting that listing. You must keep focused on the fact that **you are there to convince (persuade!!!!!) them that you can provide them with what they NEED**. At this point it is too easy to **NOT** put pressure on these people if they defer signing the listing. The untrained salesperson, at this point, can easily think that by being nice, and leaving without the signatures, they will certainly get the call tomorrow to have you come back for the listing. Well, folks...... it ain't gonna happen!

"We Have To Think About It."

How many times have you heard, **"Well, it sounds good, but we really do have to think about it?"** Or, my favorite, **"Well, we really do owe it to the other two that are coming**

later to hear what they have to say." Don't let them off like that. Don't let them get off that easily!! Why are you there? To leave them a book? To give them an appraisal? No. You are there for the listing. You have spent HOURS getting to this point, so what's another hour, more or less?

So.........................

Now you have an opportunity to have some real fun. This is **SELLING!**

Your List of Closes

Always be prepared for any refusal. Write down as many reasons as you can think of which they could possibly come up with that would put off signing that listing contract. Always remember this: Saying "NO" only means that your prospects have not received enough information yet to make their decision. And we know that the correct decision is that you are the **ONLY LOGICAL CHOICE** to list their property:

Here are the most common refusals:

1.   **"Well, we really do owe it to the others who have made appointments"**

Answer: "Mr. & Mrs. Jones, we have gone over the entire marketing plan of how **WE** are going to sell your property. From today, when I take the *For Sale* sign out of my trunk and put it on your lawn - till the day we open escrow - you have worked out every step during these past 2 hours. We even went over what my qualifications are for doing this job. Is there **ANYTHING** which you feel you would find in another Realtor which would give you more? If anything, the best you would find is exactly what we have agreed upon here, and I'm sure you don't want to spend another two to four hours hearing the same thing. Would you agree with that?" **(At this point - SHUT UP!!)**

What Mr. & Mrs. Jones will probably say at this time is, "Oh, you have given a wonderful presentation." "But, we did make those appointments to hear the other people."

2.   **"Well, we did make the appointments."**

Answer: "Yes you did, and I'm sure you don't want to offend anyone, but the fact is, you can select only one person to do this job for you, and that means that the others will be left out. This has happened to me before, and these people are strangers to you just as I was before I got here, right?" **WAIT FOR THE ANSWER** (If the answer to this question is, "No, they're not strangers," we have another close for this objection later.) "Well, Mr. & Mrs. Jones, let me tell you this little story about something that happened to me about a year ago and I really feel that it fits right into this situation. I love telling this story, because I was in basically the same situation you are in right here."

The Story Of Spencer

I had sold a home to this couple, Bob and Penny Stevers and, as is customary, they hired a licensed contractor to inspect the home. One of the items mentioned in the inspection was that the garage door did not roll up. Well, Bob and Penny told me that that garage door **had to be in working order at the close of escrow** because they planned to move quite a bit of their belongings into the garage because they were going to do some renovations before actually moving in. So we requested for that item to be repaired. The owner's agent mentioned that his seller was very adamant about the fact that the home was sold in it's **"As Is"** condition, and that that was the reason he had accepted such a low price. This was a very small problem, when looked at as part of the whole picture, but my buyers were getting very excited about that garage door! So, I told them that I would take care of this tiny detail, and that they should relax and go down to

Starbuck's and have a cup of coffee. Good grief! Buyers get so emotional!!

Always Get Three Estimates??

So, I called three garage door shops and set up times, half an hour apart, to meet the repairmen at the home to get their estimates. *Always get three estimates, right?* Well, the first guy showed up dressed up in a tan work suit with his name patch, Spencer, right above the pocket. He had a beard, long hair, and I couldn't help noticing that his hands were scarred from years of toiling on garage doors. But he was quite clean. After he introduced himself to me, and gave me his card, he said, "Okay, let's take a look at this door," and we walked back to the garage and went in the side door.

1) He looked the door over from top to bottom and from left to right.
2) He examined the roller tracks on both sides and then grabbed a box and slid it over below where the springs were.
3) He stepped up on the box and closely examined those springs, and grunted a little bit.
4) Then he asked me to step up on the box and "take a look at them springs." "Pretty rusty, eh?"
5) Then he took this wire brush out of his pocket, got up on the box, and vigorously rubbed the springs with the brush, causing dust and rust to go flying everywhere.
6) He then grunted again, got down and told me that he would not have to replace the springs because he could clean and oil them and that would "save some money." (This was a nice FAB job on me, and I took note.)
7) Then, getting me involved, asked me to hold one end of his tape measure and he walked off the width of the door, took the pencil from behind his ear, and jotted

something down on his note pad. (Very clever, thought I.)

8) Then he asked me to hold the tape measure at the top of the door and he measured the height of the door, jotting this down as well.

9) Then he looked at the roller tracks again, and pointed out that one side was quite bent.

10) Next he grabbed this cable that had apparently been attached to something on the door and showed me the end of the cable, where it had obviously snapped. "Must have been a lot of stress on this wire to make it snap like this." I agreed, of course.

11) He noted that the door itself was in pretty good shape by tapping it in several places with his screw driver.

12) Next, he asked me to wait a minute while he went out to his truck to "get something."

By now we had been fooling around back in this filthy garage for about 15 minutes. When he came back he had two sections of roller tracks, which he tested against the rollers on this particular door. After grunting a few more times, and jotting down something else on his note pad, he began figuring something on a form which I guessed to be a "Work Order," or a "Job Estimate." After about a minute, he said, "How does One Hundred Thirty Sound?"

To tell you the truth, I did not know if that job was worth sixty bucks or three hundred sixty. But the fact is, *it wasn't* three hundred sixty, it was one hundred thirty, and that amount seemed reasonable for the repair of that door.

So, what did I do at this point? That's right. The classic: **"I've got two more guys coming over to give me bids, so I'll have to get back to you**." Now, as I have described Spencer to you, he was not a slick, professional, salesman type of a guy, if you get my drift. But what he said was very slick.

Knowing that with two more guys coming over to give me bids, his chance of getting the job was probably pretty slim. But

Spenc had *sized me up* pretty good. So, he looked me dead in the eye and said, "**Do you really want to hear this all again?**" And then he **SHUT UP!** There I was, dressed up in a white shirt and tie, standing inside some dusty garage, and Spencer had hit the problem right on: **I DID NOT HAVE TIME FOR THIS!!!** He had just provided me with everything I needed to know about getting this job done, and a quote for completion at a reasonable price. What else did I need?????? I surely did not need to waste anymore time. Spencer had demonstrated to me that he was perfectly capable of doing this job that I needed to get done, and in fact, had just done as beautiful a sales job on me as any I had ever done on any prospect since I had been a salesman. He had identified my need, provided a solution, and allowed me a way to solve my problem at a reasonable cost!! It was beautiful.

I looked at Spencer, and he looked at me, and we both kind of chuckled and I said, "Okay Spenc, when can you do it?" He said, "Just give me 24 hours leeway and I can do the whole thing in about 3 to 3 ½ hours," while at the same time giving me the work order and his pen.

As we were walking out to his truck, the 2nd garage door guy was pulling up in his van so I had to go over to tell him I was sorry, but I had decided that I was going to have the job done by "that guy over there." He wasn't very happy about it, but what could he say? Then I grabbed my cell phone and called the other guy and canceled the meeting, catching him just before he left his shop. **Bottom line was, I didn't know these other guys, and I really didn't care about them. I cared about myself and I did not feel like wasting anymore of my valuable time.**

"**Mr. & Mrs. Jones, the reason I am telling you this story is that you are in the same situation as I was with that garage door guy.**

"**I mean, do you REALLY need to hear it all again?**

"**Don't you think that I can do this job for you?**" Once again, wait for an answer.

When they admit that "Yes, you have convinced us that you can do this job for us," tell them,

"**Mr. & Mrs. Jones, I will call the other agents and politely tell them that you have made your selection and that you have asked that I make the call to** *save them the trouble of wasting their valuable time.*

After all, you have never met them and probably never will, so you are actually doing them a favor.......*AND THEY CAN STILL SELL IT FOR YOU!!* (I love that last part.)

I would really appreciate that if someone did that for me, because I don't have TIME to waste." Once again - keep quiet. Slide the pen across the table towards them.

This little story is true, and you have my permission to use it as your own.

3. **"Well, we'd like to think about it."**

The classic procrastinator! Be ready for this one, because you will hear it a million times. **"Think about what!!!! I've told you everything you wanted to know. Now take this pen and sign that listing!!!!"** Of course, you can't really say it in these words.

Answer: **"Mr. & Mrs. Jones, I have heard that before and it usually comes from people who are very conservative and don't like to jump into things; just like the two of you."**

"Usually what I find when I am told this is that I really did not provide all the information the people were looking for during my presentation."

"Can you think of something I omitted which you wanted to know about???????"

WAIT FOR AN ANSWER! The answer will usually be a compliment on what a *fine* presentation you have just done for them.

Review Reason For Selling, Escrow Period, & Prep. Work

Then it's your turn: **"Let's see, you told me that you have to sell because of the *job transfer (or, whatever)*, we agreed on a *reasonable asking price*, we decided on *how long an escrow period* would be best for you folks, we went over *what you would be doing to prepare your property for sale*, and I agreed to *help you with the closing costs* (and, if appropriate, the commission).**
What is missing? What were you looking for that I did not have? Please, tell me."
This is a very important moment in your listing presentation. At this time, your principals should fess up to what they were looking for, to which you can easily promise to provide. But usually, they won't say *anything*, because they realize that they really don't have any reason not to sign, other than the fact that the time has finally come to decide on this very crucial matter in their lives. **Don't say anything else**. Sloooooooowly, slide the pen over to them and remain quiet.

4.   **"We really have to get going here. This has taken longer than expected."**

Answer: "We are already finished! All I have to do is complete the remainder of this agreement, and I'm out the door. It will take only 5 minutes more." After you get their signatures, you can come back later for the other disclosures. Push the pen in their direction with the contract opened to the last page, and wait. This objection is often followed by Objection # 3: "We always think things over before we sign anything." Therefore, you must revert to the solution for overcoming that objection.

5.   **"We don't like to be pressured!"**

Answer: "Mr. & Mrs. Jones, I know that you are feeling pressure. I understand that—it is my business. Selling your home after all these years is ENORMOUS pressure. But what I have tried to show you here during the past 2 hours (or, whatever) is that a lot of pressure can be eliminated by having the correct marketing plan for the sale of your property, AND the correct person handling if for you. Wouldn't you want a person like me handling this situation for you? Once again, **SHUT UP**. After a few seconds, slooooooowly slide the pen over to them.

6.   "We want to give you an 'OPEN LISTING.'"

How generous of them!!!! This is the famous FSBO and is definitely one of the most difficult objections to overcome. Sometimes, it is best to avoid FSBO's because they are FSBO's for a reason.   They think they can do it themselves, and therefore, they are smarter than any Realtor. However, we know that most FSBO's wind up listing their properties sooner or later, so if you are the type of individual who can deal with these very difficult prospects, there are ways to approach them and get an *EXCLUSIVE RIGHT TO SELL LISTING* agreement.

First, you must go into your meeting realizing that these prospects have, for some reason, little respect for those in your profession. So, that part of "sizing up" your prospects is a given. They may be looking at the 6% fee they will have to cough up to a Realtor as more than they earn in a year, or they may have a long standing disdain for Realtors from years of conversations with people who see Realtors as over paid and under worked people driving around in Cadillacs and Mercedes. Therefore, you must be especially skillful in the **WARM-UP**. Be careful not to tell them how hard you work, because they have already decided, through years of conversation with their friends, that you don't work hard at all. Your effort in the **WARM-UP** is to get them to see you as a regular person. **"May I have a glass of water?"**

You also have to dig for other possible reasons they want to do it themselves. They may have a hyper active dog. They may have heard of items being stolen when no one was home. They might be afraid of having a lock box on the door and people coming into their homes in the middle of the night. All of these can be easily overcome with explanations from a sympathetic Realtor. **Have another glass of water!!** If they ask you to sit down - remember - your "sore back" requires you to sit in a straight backed chair. **"Where's the kitchen table?"**

Another point which you must realize is that most of the time, if not all of the time, the FSBO is looking to save HALF the commission. Why else are they offering to give you an OPEN LISTING? Therefore, you are really only 3% away from the deal, right?

So, your presentation should be geared towards getting the FSBO to agree with these three premises which I call:

THE FSBO TRIANGLE CLOSE:

FSBO Buyers Are Always Looking For A "Steal."

1) Anyone who approaches them **without** Realtor representation, is either looking for a steal, or they are not qualified to purchase their property. Therefore, ask the question, **"Mr. & Mrs. Jones, why do think a person would buy from you if you have no Realtor representation?"** As before, **WAIT FOR THE ANSWER**. They must agree that MOST people who will approach them without a Realtor, will either be unqualified to buy their home and/or they are probably looking for a steal and that they will be looking to knock 6% to 10% off their asking price, **at the start! "Why else would someone look without a Realtor? They don't have to pay a Realtor to search out a home for them." What's up with this???**

FSBO Buyers Are Usually Not Qualified To Buy.

2) Many Realtors will **not** approach them with their **QUALIFIED** buyers, because they have experienced so much difficulty working with FSBO's over their years of experience, that they don't want the trouble. **"Mr. & Mrs. Jones, if you were a Real Estate person working with some qualified buyers, would you show a home to your people if there was no Realtor working on the other side? Would you be willing to do the whole deal for half price?"** WAIT. **"Perhaps you would do this if no other homes were on the market similar to the For Sale By Owner, but you would probably avoid it, don't you agree?"**

Your Services Are Worth The Other Half Of The Commission.

3) The third side of the triangle must show that the value of your services is well worth the additional 3%. In fact, why not add a few thousand dollars to the asking price, and list the property through the MLS? **"Mr. & Mrs. Jones, we could list your property through the MLS at a slightly higher price and it would immediately be exposed to all the qualified buyers within this price range. With that type of immediate exposure, don't you think that would be the best way for you to get the highest price for your home?"**

Like Talking To A Tree Stump!

The problem which I always found when working FSBO's was that they will sit there and agree with everything you say, nodding their heads in the same directions as you had been doing. But when it came time to ask for the signatures they would repeat that they would be happy to give you an OPEN LISTING!! Sometimes it's like talking to a tree stump!

FSBO's are tough, and most times they require a two stage presentation. That is, a WARM-UP on day one, and a 2nd appointment for the full, planned, step by step presentation which builds to a successful closing. It is difficult to close on the first appointment because many times there will be people wandering through the home which will disrupt the necessary continuity of the sale presentation. They will be getting up to show these "buyers" around, making sure to point out all the things about their home which they feel are important "selling features," but usually are things that nobody cares about. Like, for example, the nice shelves installed over the washer and dryer in the garage which will probably be the first things ripped out when the new owner moves in. I'm sure that those of us who have been around a while, know what I'm talking about. Rather pathetic, really. If you do work with FSBO's, it may be necessary for them to wear themselves out before they realize they need your services and the MLS.

7. **"How many houses have you sold in this neighborhood?"**

This is straight from Mr. "I Know Everything," from the Sunday Real Estate section. We, as Real Estate professionals, know that it really doesn't matter how many homes you have sold in that neighborhood, and we know that for a variety of reasons. But to tell Mr. & Mrs. Jones, "Look, that is a foolish question," would not be getting the job done. The important thing is to make them realize that you are the best one to get THEIR property sold. So, you must be prepared to respond to this objection with an answer specifically tailored to your position in the neighborhood.

Your *"FAB"*ulous Responses

A. If your company has many sales in that neighborhood, but *you have few or none*, bring a printout of all those sales and emphasize that your company's signs are well known around the neighborhood and that the local agents always enjoy working with you and other people in your office because of your professional presence. This is a feature, advantage, and benefit to Mr. & Mrs. Jones. "Don't you think I can get the job done for you?" **WAIT FOR THE ANSWER**.

B. If your company does *not* have many sales in that particular neighborhood, bring a printout of as many sales similar in price that your company has been involved in during, say the past 1 or 2 years. F.A.B. "You have seen that we do quite a bit of advertising in this area. **(Feature)** We attract many buyers in this price range with our advertising. **(Advantage)** It's just coincidence that we haven't placed a stack of them in your neighborhood." "Our company will be working harder than ever to get a sale recorded in this neighborhood. **(Benefit)**

C. If you have *not sold any homes* in their neighborhood, or their price range, it is time to bring out a few testimonials. I always carried a few letters from former clients who had been pleased with my performance in doing the transaction for them. You should have a few of these from your clients. Tell them that you did not start out selling a house the first 2 weeks, and your first deal wasn't a million dollar deal, but you started somewhere, and you have always done a good job. "Don't you think, after sitting here and talking with me for the past hour and a half, that I would do a good job for you?" "Do you have any idea how difficult it is to talk with an agent who has 10 listings and 5 escrows going at once?" "You've already agreed with me that your home is really the only one you care about, right?"

D. If you have *never sold any homes* and have *never had any listings*, you must emphasize your energy and earnestness. That's why your presentation should be sharp, detailed, and controlled. Bring print outs of sales which have been made by your company in their price range and/or neighborhood. However, the question is rarely asked, "Have you ever sold *any* houses?" Or, "How many properties have you sold?" Don't lie. If you start a pattern of lies, you will get caught - someday. Besides, it's easier to tell the truth. I don't recommend volunteering the information that this is your first deal, but that would be up to you. If you have not had any transactions yet, it might be a good idea to pair up with someone in your office. Half a deal is better than none, and the experience of a partner could rub off on you in a very positive way. Some people do quite good work in "teams." And a "team" will appear attractive to Mr. & Mrs. Jones. This would be another **FEATURE, ADVANTAGE, & BENEFIT** to the Jones'.

8.   **"We have a friend of our daughter's plumber who has a Real Estate License and we told her that we would listen to her presentation."**

This one is a tough one. Getting a listing when there is a relative, friend, or friend of a friend in the way poses several problems which are difficult to confront directly. The fact is though, that if you are there for an interview, they really haven't decided who is going to do this job for them. Therefore, there are ways to get around this situation, and still get the listing.

"Mr. & Mrs. Jones, everyone knows someone who has a real estate license. Wouldn't you agree with that? As a matter of fact, you probably know more than one person with a real estate license, right? The fact is, you are talking about probably the *biggest, and most important investment* you have. Would I be correct in making that statement? (Wait for an answer.) Now let me ask you something, and I would like for you to take a minute to envision the situation before you answer me. *What would happen if you had to fire*

your listing agent because of unsatisfactory performance and that agent was a personal friend (or relative, or whatever)? **Could you do that? It would be awkward and difficult, wouldn't it?"**

Or, worse yet, Mr. & Mrs. Jones, what if you were already *in escrow* **and things weren't going along to your satisfaction? It would be impossible to fire your agent at that time. You might be required to seek outside counsel.**

WAIT FOR AN ANSWER!

Getting them to agree with you on this matter is important. "Mr. & Mrs. Jones, let me tell you what I can offer you to help you avoid this possible ugly scenario. I've done this before, and it seems to work out quite well. If you *absolutely* feel an obligation to this person, and you agree with me that listing your property with him (or her) could develop into an uneasy situation, I will share my fee with them by using the standard referral fee which we Realtors generally swap back and forth. This will allow you to avoid having your **personal relationships** become involved in your *personal* **business**, and still allow them to receive some remuneration from your transaction. **And they can still sell it for you!!** (Don't you love that one?) That's more than fair, don't you agree?" While they are pondering your question, slooooooooooooowly slide the pen over to them.

9. **"We have at least 3 people we know very well who have Real Estate licenses."**

This one is easy. Whichever "friend" they elect to handle their listing, they are bound to offend someone. "Mr. & Mrs. Jones, that doesn't surprise me because it seems that every 3rd person in this state has a real estate license. The question I would like to ask you, and I would like for you to reflect on the situation for a moment before answering me, is if you select one of these friends, how do you think the other two will feel?"

WAIT FOR AN ANSWER!! "Mr. & Mrs. Jones, if these people are true friends, believe me, there are going to be some hurt feelings. They may never say so, but if you were in the position of one of the "losers," wouldn't you feel a little insulted?" Could you hear them saying, "Well, I guess Joe & Judy think a lot more of Mary than they think of me!" I guarantee you, they will feel that way, and I'm equally sure they will never mention it to you. Now, if you were to select someone totally outside your circle of acquaintances, such as myself, representing a strong firm, you could tell each of your friends that because it was "such a personal matter," you felt that it was necessary to select a totally independent party to represent you in the sale of your property. **"Now, doesn't that make sense?"** At the same time nodding your head in the affirmative. When they nod in agreement, what do we do? That's right—we slide the pen over to them.

10.   **"We are going to list our property on the internet."**

Your response (not answer): "Mr. & Mrs. Jones, you invited me over here this evening knowing that I was an agent with a full service real estate brokerage firm. We have sat here the past hour and a half discussing the sale of your property and I have gotten the impression that this will be a very, very important event in your lives. Am I to believe that you will entrust the marketing, buyer viewings, price negotiations, inspections, and all the other nuances of completing a safe transaction for the sale of your property to **an internet device without a face?"**

Mr. & Mrs. Jones will probably respond that their concern is that **"you just cost too much."** (Remember, this one is only about COST.)

Are You People Cadillac People, Or Volkswagen People?

Your response: (Pause for a moment, as if carefully forming a thoughtful response.) "Of course our cost is more. It is much more. But you must admit that any service you receive has a cost to it. Mr. & Mrs. Jones, let me use this analogy, and let me say that it is an extreme example, but bear with me a moment: **If you got the tragic news that one of you needed a new heart, or kidney, or whatever, would you look for the least expensive human organ to solve your problem?**" At this point, let them reflect on that statement for a moment. If they do not speak in a moment or so, make the statement that you hope they are thinking to themselves: **"All things cost money, Mr. & Mrs. Jones, it just comes down to whether you want the Cadillac or the Volkswagen Bug."**

The fact is, ladies and gentlemen, that this objection is a tough one. More and more advertising is done for these internet companies, and to the uninformed client, they sound very good. I mean, who *wouldn't* want to save thousands of dollars when they sell their homes? But the fact is this: if these people have gone as far as scheduling an appointment with you to discuss the sale of their home, they have some doubts about whether the internet is the way to go. It is your opportunity to reinforce their doubts about selecting an internet service to sell their property and to educate them on the real benefits of the personalized service which you, the Real Estate professional, will provide them.

If You Are There.....................

This is a very tough sale, so the value of a prepared, rehearsed presentation, with you sitting across the table as the knowledgeable, professional advisor, will be all the more necessary in gaining the confidence of these property owners. Remember what we talked about earlier: if you are there, they have not decided.   So persistence on your part will be imperative.

11.   "We're not signing anything tonight, and that's that!!!!"

Your answer, with a most pensive look on your face, is **"You are not going to sign anything tonight....................unless?????"** Once again, remain quiet. This is an opportunity for Mr. Jones to express to you what he has been searching for in your presentation, but you have failed to demonstrate. Remember, you are sitting across the table from him at his request. He wants to sell his property. You are his avenue to successfully solving this problem for him. Whatever his response, you will have the opportunity at this time to provide a solution to his final requirement.

If you cannot get your prospects to agree with you on any of these closes, remain affable and talkative.   Engage them in conversation.   Sometimes, after a long time sitting around talking with them, they will ask you,

12.   "Mary, *when* are you going to leave?"

Your answer, with the biggest smile you can make on your face, is **"Not till you sign the listing."** Once again, slide the pen over to them. If you have built a good rapport with these people, and spent a long time at the table with them going through your entire presentation in the prepared manner, this should finally do it. You might even say, **"Mr. & Mrs. Jones, wouldn't you like to have me on *your side* of the table when an offer comes in?"**

When all of the above closes have not produced the signatures on the agreement, there is still one last thing which you can do.

13.   **The "COLUMBO" Close**

There is one last close which I use when they have put you off on your last close, **"Not till you sign this listing."** I call this *"The Columbo Close."* Acting as if you are defeated, you should start to pack up all your materials and put them into your case. This will relieve the pressure on them which they have been experiencing while resisting your closes. The "Contract" is packed away. Their defenses will relax. They are "safe." As you begin to leave the table and walk towards the door, still being conversational, take two steps and stop. Then, in your most affable manner, ask, **"By the way, Mr. & Mrs. Jones, what was the real reason you would not sign the listing this evening?"** With the pressure off, most of the time they will tell you the one thing that was holding them back. With that last bit of information, you can now say, **"Oh my God, didn't I tell you about that?"** while at the same time sitting back down at the table and opening your case. **"Let's go over that and let me show you how we can handle it for you."**

This would be your final attempt at closing the deal. If you have gotten this far without them agreeing to sign the listing, your prospects should be so exhausted that this final close should have them agreeing that it would make no sense *"NOT"* to sign your contract. Your presentation, if it has gone this far, should have uncovered every possible objection and provided reasonable solutions for each.

If your prospects have not been persuaded to sign your listing contract after all of this time, you can at least feel confident that you have done a thorough and complete presentation. When you leave you should have worked up a good sweat and hopefully, your prospects will have the same feelings. They should be so tired, they won't want to see anyone else.

So, let's wrap up this section on listing presentations before we begin the section on buyers.

The Six Premises of Sales

There are *Six Premises* which we can keep in mind when we are about to make a **SALES** presentation:

1)   Good Salesmanship = AAP (Appearance, Attitude, & Preparation)
2)   People buy from people they like.
3)   Only one person is going to get the deal, so it might as well be you.
4)   Most people only care about one thing: themselves.
5)   "NO" means, "I need more information."
6)   The prospect is not a *friend* until he signs the contract.

That's a pretty short list of what you need to keep in mind when you are doing business. But if you incorporate them into your habits when you "go to work," you will find that you will be more successful in your business. And when that happens - we all have a lot more fun doing what we do.

If you rehearse your presentation, deliver it in the order you have planned, and be ready for your prospects when they say "NO," you will do great. Train yourselves to do it right and don't be afraid to practice. You'll discover that you will become polished in your presentation and that you will be getting PAID for your preparations. Isn't it a great feeling when you are driving away from a listing presentation and you have the signatures on the listing contract and your sign is in the front lawn?

Larry Hauser

PART II

Working With Buyers

Where Are They & What Are They??

The second part of this book will be a discussion about how to handle buyers. First of all, where do we, as Real Estate **SALES** people, get buyers? Buyers are everywhere. But, it's a fact; there are "Buyers" and there are "**Buyers**." The difference is, of course, which "buyer" will actually *buy*. It is so easy to become involved with people who act like buyers, but who, for various reasons, do not buy. **How many agents have worked with a "buyer" for 3 months and not gotten paid for it?** The number is too large to measure. It happens all the time. As we go on, I'm going to give you a "*PLAN*" which you can implement into your own style which will help you weed out the NON-Buyers from the **Buyers**. By following the steps I will give you for your *PLAN*, you will *reduce the waste of time* which erodes all of your incomes.

"Uh,……..We Bought Another House"

Is there anything more devastating in the Real Estate business than to have worked with so called "*buyers*" for a long period of time and then one day notice that they are not returning your calls? Hmmmmm? Then finally you get them to pick up the phone and they mumble and stumble and you discover that they have purchased a house from another Realtor, or worse, from a FSBO. Just thinking about it makes me sick. It happened to me many times in my early years in the business. But as time went by I learned, by trial and error, when to avoid certain types of people and when to "lock in" on others. As you read on, you will learn how to avoid this "time trap" if you follow my plan.

How To Qualify The *"Buyer"*

We have all heard the rule, "**Qualify your buyer.**" **But what does that mean exactly?** Does that mean that as soon as you meet someone at an open house, or from an up-call, that you ask them to produce their credentials to prove to you that they can afford to purchase what you are about to show them? That would be a good idea, if we could get away with it, but most people get real cranky if you ask them what they earn before you are two minutes into the initial conversation. So, you have to get to that information in a round about manner.

Necessary Steps To The Successful Offer Presentation

I

Present Yourself

First, let it be obvious to the *"Buyer"* that you are a professional. Depending upon where you do your business, dress is very important. Beach people, or those in rural areas, can get away with casual clothes. Actually, casual dress is best in these types of areas. Upscale communities require different attire. Perhaps a blue or white shirt and tie for the guys, skirts and blouses for the ladies. Be careful not to over do it, but always be clean and neat. I have always tried to be just a little bit better dressed than the people I was meeting. Believe me, the old adage, *"first impressions are the most important"* holds true. There have been so many studies regarding the effects of first impressions, that you probably could not read them all in a year. That first hand shake and first eye contact will determine how you will be accepted by your prospects.

So, by starting with care in your appearance, you have projected a professional image to your prospective buyers and this will help them to feel confident that you can handle the difficult process of finding them the "perfect" property. You want them to feel that you are the person who can guide them through all the difficult procedures necessary to close the deal. And ideally, you want them to feel that you are the **BEST** choice for them to complete this step in their lives.

Larry Hauser

II

Buyer Qualification

The Four Qualifying Questions:

This discussion is not about where to get buyers, because every rookie training class has a part for that. Open Houses, Up-Calls, Calls From Your Own Ads, Asking the *"BIG Question"*, etc., etc. The four important things which the *trained salesperson* must determine are:

1) is this "buyer" **able** to buy?
2) is this "buyer" **willing** to buy?
3) **when** does this "buyer" want to buy?
4) **what** can this "buyer" actually buy?

Simply put, these four questions determine the *QUALIFICATIONS* of the prospect, and will determine whether or not you will spend time with these people.

So, step number two in building towards a successful offer presentation is *BUYER QUALIFICATION*.

But, how can you, in a very unobtrusive way, determine if these "buyers" are worthy of your time?

Let me briefly discuss "Up-Time," because that is one way to get "buyers."

I'm sure there is not one person in the Real Estate business who has **not** had "Up-Time" at one time or another. Therefore, we have all spent time taking calls on ads for listed properties. Have you ever noticed how some people are a lot more successful with up-time than others? Why is that? Well, it's obvious that it has to do with the way they speak with people who call in, wouldn't you agree?

80

The Five Primary Reasons Why People Call Real Estate Offices

I have found that most of the calls coming into the up desk are not going to take you anywhere. There are 5 primary reasons why people call into Real Estate offices:

1) The first is the call from a person who is already working with a Realtor. That call probably is going nowhere.

2) Next is some individual who just saw a sign go up in his neighborhood and wants to know what his friend "Joe" is asking for his house. Another nowhere call. But possibly a seller down the road, so make an attempt to get information for your card file.

3) "Mary," who very good naturedly, is just checking for her son, or daughter, or somebody else who will find their own Realtor and is just wasting your time. Be polite, but cut this person loose quickly.

4) The individual who is looking for a rental or lease, and may in the future be a buyer. It's your choice as to whether or not to spend any time with this caller.

5) And lastly, the person who might be just beginning to look for a home, or is moving into the area from elsewhere and sooner, or later, will connect with a Realtor, so it might as well be you.

So, admittedly, most of the calls that come into the "Up-Desk" are worthless. But if you take the "Up-Time" you know that. It's a numbers game, so you take the calls. I'm not going to beat this to death, because I know that everyone has their own style on the phone, and I have not written this book to tell you how to speak with people on the phone. I've written this book to help you become **PROFICIENT IN SELLING**, and to learn how to **STOP WASTING TIME.**

III

Determining If The Buyer Is A "Buyer"

To reduce your *wasted time*, you must have a plan on how you are going to handle the "Up-Call." First, if any of the callers fall into one of the first four categories I have listed, you must realize that you're not going to get paid for any work you do for these people, so be as brief as possible with these callers. Dump them. Be polite, of course, but get rid of them. These people will ask you to show them property, send them lists of homes for sale, etc., but the fact is, your work will be for nothing.

Nine Questions Which Must Be Answered

The last category listed is from someone who needs help, and it is your choice, as well as the caller's, as to whether or not you can form a working relationship. So, with these callers, you must have a *plan*. And the plan is, very simply, a list of questions which you must interject into your telephone conversation to determine if the caller is worthy of your time.

1) **Are you working with a Realtor now?**
2) **Are you renting now, or do you own a home?**
3) **Where do you live now?**
4) **Have you spoken with any lenders to find out where you should be as far as monthly payments go? (Another way of asking, *"Have you been pre-qualified?"*)**
5) **How much do you have saved for your down payment?**
6) **In what form is the down payment? (Stocks, cash, IRA, etc.)**
7) **How many bedrooms do you need?**

8) **What's most important to you about the home you buy?**
9) **What is your telephone number?**

I cannot tell you how to conduct your telephone conversations, but I can tell you that you *must* get this information from the prospect if you are going to *avoid wasting time*. If you can't get this information from them, they probably aren't really interested in buying a home and you can separate the "non-buyer" from the "probable buyer" right then. Those who have a lot of experience with up-time know that some people will be more than willing to chat with you on the phone, and others just want a few answers to their questions and are not willing to give any information about themselves. Because it is a telephone conversation, it is very difficult to control the relationship at this early stage. So, admittedly it is merely a numbers game with up-time.

Arrange A Face To Face Meeting

So, because we can't control the prospects at this point, your objective is to determine as much about the individual as possible so that you can make a decision as to whether it is worthwhile to go further. If your questioning has provided enough "qualifying" information to deem this caller worthy of your time, your next objective is to get the caller to come into your office to meet with you. **Only by meeting face to face can the caller gain respect for you as a professional.** The caller must be convinced that you are the one who can assist them in locating the "perfect" home which they are seeking.

I'm sure that everyone who has had experience at up-time will agree that until you have a face to face meeting with a caller, you will not be successful in gaining a working relationship with that person. I found that by asking them very early on if they would like to come to your office to view some listings, speak with your mortgage broker, have a glass of water, ANYTHING, to get them to come to your office to meet with you, is the only way in which you will be able to get a working relationship with them. If they have a home to sell, see if you can think up some scheme to go over to their house and meet them. Or perhaps, you can arrange to meet them at an open house in a day or two. *Remember, you only have a chance with these up-calls if you can arrange a face to face meeting so that they connect your voice with a real live person.* So, the sooner you can do that, the better. And therefore, less of your valuable time will be wasted. Does that make some sense?

As I mentioned, this book was not written as an instruction as to how to get buyers. I leave that to your basic training classes. This book is about becoming **Proficient in Selling and How to Stop Wasting Time.**

The next objective is perhaps the most difficult in all of the Real Estate business:

IV

How Do We Get The Buyers To Sign A Contract?

This objective is made more difficult because most agents are afraid to ask the buyers to sign a Buyer's Contract. Am I right about that? We are too afraid that we might lose them. Well, what's worse, losing "buyers" before we have spent a month, or two, **or three** showing them around and then having them wander into an open house some day and buy from another Realtor, or a FSBO, ...or losing them before we have spent a lot of time on them? So, how do you, as a group of professionals, get this contract signed?

The answer is really quite simple: **YOU ASK FOR IT**! You are salespeople and surely must agree that you don't get anything unless you ask for it. The problem is, how do you ask a buyer to sign your contract without scaring off those *REAL* buyers?

The Big Question To Mr. & Mrs. Buyer:

How about this: "Okay Mr. & Mrs. Jones, when can you come down to my office so we can sign some papers authorizing me to do this work for you? *That way you'll know you have an agent and I'll know I have a client—okay?*"

That's a pretty simple request, wouldn't you agree? It doesn't sound too threatening. And yet, we are scared to death to ask that question. This is the *DEMAND* which is made by lawyers before they do *ANY* work for clients. And they always get the signatures before they even consider doing anything for clients. Contractors do the same thing. Even Spencer, the crafty garage door guy I mentioned earlier, had me sign his contract. Do you remember that? He *ASKED* me to sign it and I decided that if I wanted this work to get done, I would naturally be required to sign something. So, when do *you*, the Real Estate professional, ask this question? How can you fit this into your

SALES PRESENTATION to your buyers so that it appears to be the normal thing to do?

Avoid Being Stung

Sometime, early in your relationship with your "buyers" you should make the attempt to get the Buyers' Contract signed so that you can avoid being stung a month or two, (or three) later. I have found that after asking all the qualifying questions which we went over earlier, and determining that these are *REAL* buyers, that it is imperative to pin these people down with a commitment. I don't feel that it is an unreasonable request to ask for this commitment from buyers, so we must make the request seem like a natural way of doing business.

Instill Confidence In The Buyer

Of course, you would not expect them to commit to you before they actually felt confident in your abilities of doing this job for them, so you must go through the necessary "sales" steps to gain their confidence. Sometimes, *in fact most times*, it should be arranged to show them one or two houses which might be appealing to them and priced within their price range. **But be careful that you don't get trapped into spending too much time in this process before you get the signatures on the Buyers' Contract.** If you spend too much time early on without those signatures, they will get the impression that it is okay to have you do all this work without any commitment on their part. It is very easy to get into this trap, and I've done it more than a few times, so take the effort to do a good warm-up and then ask the question: **"When can you come over to my office to sign some papers authorizing me to do this work for you? That way you'll know you have an agent, and I'll know I have a client, okay?"**

Train Yourselves To Get The Buyers' Contract Signed

If enough Real Estate sales people use this practice of getting signatures on Buyers' Contracts everyone will be working much more effectively, and at the same time looking much more professional. So, as a professional, start thinking about how you can work this technique into your approaches with buyers. Once again, you have to *train* yourselves to do these different things, but in the long run, it will be very beneficial, I'm sure you'll agree.

Don't Let The Buyers Take The Contract For "Review."

One way we can still beat ourselves with this *"NEW"* concept of asking for signatures on the Buyers' Contract is to allow the buyer to take the contract with them to *"Review."* If you give your buyers this contract to take with them, you will most likely never hear from them again. First of all, this contract is quite lengthy, so they will do what most people do: they will procrastinate. At best, the contract will lie on their kitchen table so that they can "review" it when they get a chance. At worst, and most probably, they will call one of their friends, or one of your competitors, and they will be told that it is not necessary to sign any contract if they are "just looking" and that Suzie, from ABC Realty, will be happy to drive them around and show them houses until she is an old lady, or until they find one they like. Whichever one comes first.

Remember: You Are A Professional.

So, because you have projected yourself to these people as a professional sales person, you must explain to them that it is a very detailed contract and that you want to be there to go over it with them. **DON'T GIVE IN!!!** Remember, you are *finished* if they take this contract with them to review! Try your best to sit down with them right then and there. But, if you cannot get them to spend time with you right then to review that contract, then try this:

"**Mr. & Mrs. Jones, if you don't have time to spend right now to go over this contract, why don't we set a time when we can do it together. I've been doing this a long time and I know from experience that people always have questions when they go through this contract so I like to be there with them when they do.** *This is pretty important, wouldn't you agree?* **(WAIT FOR THE RESPONSE.) How about if I swing by your place this evening (or whenever). (If they live far enough away as to make it illogical for you to appear at their home, then you must be forceful about getting them into your office to review the contract with you.)**

Don't blow it.

Force yourself to realize how important it is to get this contract signed at this stage of your association with these buyers. If you have done the proper preparation with these buyers as I have illustrated, you have in your hands a valuable commodity. *Don't blow it.* A signed "Buyers' Contract" will almost guarantee payment for your efforts, and prevent what often happens with "loose" buyers: huge amounts of wasted time and not even a "thank you" from these people when they buy a house through another Realtor.

If these "*buyers*" deflect your efforts to get them to agree to the "Buyers' Contract," these buyers are expecting your services free of charge and as a consequence, will really have no respect for you or the time you spend on their behalf.

What To Do When You Find That "*Perfect*" Home.

So, what to do when you find the perfect home for your buyer? This usually takes an enormous amount of work, wouldn't you agree? It takes a lot of your time, which incidentally, the buyers actually never know about the *real* time you spend "previewing" homes for them and checking the new listings. So, when this "perfect" home is identified, and your buyers agree to write an offer, why not do everything possible to make sure that you get the deal, right?

The Ron *"I Love Myself"* Story

Let me relate this little story to you. It happened right before my eyes.

An agent in my office, Helen Banos, had been having no results with her listing of a beautiful townhome in South Redondo Beach, California. She had had it on the market for 3 weeks and had not had a single offer. Her sellers were considering lowering their asking price of $459,000 to $445,000 because they wanted to get on with their plans. Helen had received many calls from agents who had previewed the property, and there had been numerous showings. However, there had been no offers.

So, one afternoon while we were working in the office, a call came in from a Realtor, Ron, who told her that he had an offer and would like to come by with the offer. Now, it so happens that I knew Ron from over the years and I knew that he had been doing business in the area for probably as long as I had. He had plenty of experience in the business. In fact, years ago, he and I had worked in the same office. So, I told Helen that I would bet her it would be a low offer, and I was surprised, knowing Ron the way I did, that he had not just faxed over the offer. Maybe Ron just needed to take a little drive that day.

He Just Dropped Off His Offer

About half an hour later, Ron showed up at our office and went into the conference room with Helen to discuss the offer from his clients. After about 10 minutes, Ron left and Helen came out with the offer. Sure enough, the offer was for $420,000 which was pretty low, but in actuality, it was the

ONLY offer written on that property. Helen told me that Ron had presented his buyers' pre-qualification letter, and stated that there were no contingencies of a down-leg sale. In essence, a really clean offer. He didn't mention that his buyers would like to have a counter-offer, nor did he say that this was the best offer he could get from his buyers. He simply gave the offer to Helen, which was a pretty straight forward offer, I'm sure you will agree.

Now, what do you think Helen did at this time? Did she call her sellers and tell them that she finally had an offer? Of course, she did. But **FIRST** she called two agents who had shown the property twice to their buyers and who had conversed with her on the phone about the listing. She did her job, ladies and gentlemen!! She told the other two agents that she had an offer on the table, and that if their buyers had a serious interest in the property, they should not waste anymore time if they were interested in buying that townhome. This is called "Shopping The Offer," and I am sure everyone in the sales business has experienced this method either from the seller side or the buyer side.

After contacting the other two agents, she ***THEN*** called her sellers, who incidentally, were out of town on vacation, but were readily accessible by their telephone and a fax machine. After telling her sellers about the offer and the offer price, she mentioned that she had called the other two Realtors who had shown the property twice and that perhaps, (*MAYBE)*, there might be another offer later on. Her sellers informed her that they would counter the offer of $420,000 at $445,000 if they did not receive another offer within 24 hours, and that they would be eagerly awaiting her call within that time.

In Comes Mickey

But, sure enough, that evening one of those other Realtors, Mickey of Redondo Beach, called her and said that he had an offer and would like to get together with her and her sellers. I was not available to see how this part of the story went, but Helen told me that he came to the office and requested that she get the sellers on the phone with a conference call so that he could present his offer to them. If not in person, he could at least be perceived by her sellers in a way in which they would be able to hear that he was an actual human being. That was a pretty reasonable request, wouldn't you agree?

The other offer was for $445,000, no sale contingencies, with the same 10% down payment. How nifty for the sellers!! Now they had *TWO* offers, whereas 6 hours before, they had none and were considering lowering their price. *Now*, what do you think their counter offer was? That's right! Full price to both with the option left to the sellers to select the one they preferred.

Mickey Was In - Ron Was Retired To The Showers

Well, as it turned out, Mickey's people accepted the full price counter offer, and Ron's people couldn't make up their minds in time. Isn't it amazing how Real Estate works? Within hours the value of that property went from $445,000 to $459,000. That's 3%. But the fact is, and we all know this, the value of any property at any given time is what someone is willing to pay for it at that time.

Don't Allow Your Offer To Be "Shopped"

The moral of this story is that Ron, because of his lackadaisical manner of doing business, blew it for his buyers and in turn, wasted a lot of his own time. What Ron should have done, with what he knew was the only offer written for that property in 3 weeks, was to demand to present that offer to the sellers over the phone and request a response right then and there. If the sellers could not be reached right away, he should not have revealed the details of his offer until Helen could contact her sellers. He allowed his offer to be "*shopped*" and thereby, weakened his position. Yes, Helen could still have requested some time for her sellers to "think it over," but Ron, with good salesmanship and a smile on his face (it comes through on the phone too, ya know), could have reasoned with the sellers that his buyers really would like to have a response right away because they had been burned, or whatever, on another occasion. Depending on the ability or desires of his buyers, he could have fashioned either a counter offer or an acceptance on the spot if he had done a **SALES** job.

Don't Be Weak If You Are Coming From Strength

But Ron was *WEAK*, and as a consequence, he wasted his time writing that offer and driving over to "hand" it to Helen. Isn't it a fact that when Ron came in with that offer it was the *ONLY* offer written on that property at that time? That is *STRENGTH!!* If he had played his cards properly, he probably could have walked out of that office with a counter offer for $445,000!!! Instead, he was back at square one with his buyers. Maybe they stuck with him, or maybe they didn't. But the fact is, he had a deal when he walked into the office and he walked out with a wish. And we all know what we have when we have a wish, right? If you don't know, then let me tell you. If you have a wish in one hand, and you-know-what in the other, what do you have when you clap your hands together? That's right. You have two hands full of you-know-what.

So, remember this little story when you are presenting your offers. *Present* your offers to the sellers whenever possible and enhance the possibility that you will be paid for your efforts.

Here are some tips which I think you will agree will assist you in getting your offers accepted.

V

Finding The Right Property

Remember earlier our discussion about how people like to buy from people they like? Well, the same holds true with many sellers. *They like to sell their properties, especially their homes, to people they like.* They may not admit it, but it generally holds true. It doesn't hold true with all sellers, but you have to agree that, because a home is a very personal thing, a lot of emotion is frequently involved. Therefore, getting an offer *written* is only part of the project. There are several steps to follow before actually getting the offer written.

VI

Preparing The Sellers

Many times when you are previewing properties for your buyers, you have an opportunity to strike up a conversation with the owners. This is your chance to "sell" yourself to these people. Do a warm-up. You are a salesperson, and you naturally love conversing with people. By nature, you are gregarious. If you think that the home could be "the" one for your buyers, have a nice conversation with these owners. *How about a glass of water?* Pick out an item and admire it, just as if this couple was a potential listing possibility. ***Be careful not to get into conversation about prices***, because that comes later, and of course, it would really be quite unethical at this point without their representative being there. We're not talking about playing "*dirty*" here. Your objective at this point is to get these people to feel comfortable with you so that when you bring back an offer that is not "perfect in every way," you will be able to work *something* out with them and their agent. When you leave, they should feel good that they have had this little "chat" with this nice Real Estate person. And that's what we all are, right? Nice, friendly REAL ESTATE PEOPLE.

The *Hot Dog* Warm-Up

I remember once, several years ago, I had been working with this couple in their mid-fifties for about 6 weeks trying to find that "perfect" home for them. One came on the market one day which I felt was just right for them. It had 7 or 8 of the qualities which we had listed as necessary for them to be satisfied. However, I had made two trips to the home myself for "previewing" and had brought them there twice, but had never been there when the owners were home. Now, as I mentioned to you, with this sales procedure, *if possible*, it is necessary for you to make contact with the owners of the subject property before you bring them an offer. It isn't a technique which can be used in all cases, but listen to how I worked this and decide if you could fit it to any of your offer presentations.

Get As Much Information As You Can

My buyers wanted to take a drive down to Orange County that afternoon and think it over during the day. I was fairly confident that they were going to ask me to write an offer for them, so I contacted the agent and asked him if he could tell me anything about his sellers. He was a good agent, I thought, and he told me that it was a divorce situation and that he had been friends with this guy since the 8th grade. This, of course, was helpful information. However, I felt that I could enhance my position if I had some opportunity to speak personally with one of the owners. Call it confidence in myself, if you will. But remember, I know I'm a salesman and I love this game.

I Was Treated To Some Very Tasty Hot Dogs

So, I waited until about 5:00 o'clock to call over to the house and the owner picked up the phone. I mentioned to him that I had been over to his home twice with some people whom, I *cautiously* mentioned, seemed "fairly interested," but they had asked me to come back and take a look underneath the redwood deck which he had built in the back yard to see how it was secured in the ground. I was careful not to have him detect that my buyers were "very" interested in his property. So, he told me, "Sure - come on over."

When I got there I did my "warm-up" job of complimenting him on the fine work he had done on that deck, "and by golly, those concrete pilings aren't ever going to move." Next thing I knew was that we were sitting on the deck and he was cooking hot dogs on the grill for me and his kids and telling me all the work he had done on that house over the past 10 years. **A**

perfect warm-up! I was there for almost an hour until I got a call on my cell phone from my buyers. Sure enough, they had decided on making an offer and wanted to meet me to write it up.

You Don't Have An Offer Till It's Written

Conveniently, the seller was right there when I got the call so I told him to call his agent and tell him what had happened. But, I made it plain that there is no offer until it is written, and even though he had heard the conversation, I told him that I never say I have an offer until it is in my hand with a check.

Later, I met with my buyers, wrote up the offer, called his agent and arranged for the presentation the next evening. It was substantially less than full price - but because I had done this nifty warm-up with the seller, I was not perceived as a "bad guy" trying to steal his property. We worked out a *"Reasonable"* counter offer which my buyers found acceptable and at the close of escrow, everyone was satisfied. Mission accomplished!

VII

Buyer Meets Seller

Another sales strategy which is very beneficial to your offer process is getting your buyers into the house when the owners are there. Now, a lot of agents and brokers will think this is a horrible strategy and will reel back in shock and horror when I explain it, but here is how it is done.

First of all, the sellers will see the people who are going to be buying this most personal possession of theirs: their home. If your buyers are the type who are a little course around the edges, do some prep work on them. Tell them the strategy. Make sure they know your precept that *"people like to sell to people they like!"* This tactic doesn't always work, so be selective. However, keep in mind that you have done an enormous amount of work by this time in finding a home which your buyers are excited about buying, so don't take the easy way home. Because sometimes, you don't *get* home at all, if you get my drift.

After you have devised some way for your buyers to meet the sellers and have a little chat, remember to coach your people about not getting too specific about their liking of the property. If the sellers think your buyers are too "locked into" their home, they may get a little cocky with their response to your offer. Have your people ask some "vanilla" type questions, such as, "How are the schools?" Or, "Is there very much traffic on this street." Or, one of my favorites, "How is the plumbing?" No matter how good or how bad the plumbing is, no one ever falls in love with the plumbing. It's a good question, though. The idea with this strategy is to get a short dialog going between your buyers and the sellers so they can see that they are *real* people; just like they were when they bought the home. Make **SURE** that your people know they should not ask anything about price. That's *your* job, and you'll handle it for them.

VIII

Arranging To Present The Offer

As illustrated earlier, when I related the story of my friend Helen Banos and the offer which she received on her listing, it's really important to present your offer in person. So, after you have had this short "meeting" between your buyers and the sellers, **you must make every effort possible to arrange to present the offer in person.** As amazed as I have been over the years at sales people who open up their listing presentations with the statement that they "will do it for such and such amount," I am *doubly* amazed at sales agents who work so long and so hard to get an offer written, and then feel okay about faxing over the offer to the listing agent!! ***Aren't we all sales people!!!!*** How can you possibly *"sell"* something with a faxed presentation? Only when all else has failed, should you acquiesce to a faxed offer presentation.

So, therefore, let's discuss the offer presentation scene.

IX

The *"Offer Presentation"*

All Parties On Title Should Be Present

First, as with the listing presentation, you must make sure all parties on title are there, *if possible.* Unlike the listing presentation scene, you cannot refuse to present the offer if all parties are not present. It might be a divorce situation, or one party may be out of town, or whatever. **When you have a written offer, you must get it presented as soon as possible.** You never know what the listing agent might have, so you cannot waste time getting the offer in front of the sellers.

Dress For Business - A Must

When you arrive, of course be in respectable dress for this important occasion. A dress shirt and tie, perhaps with the collar loosened, for the guys, and something comparable for the ladies. Whatever, dress for the occasion. We want the sellers and their agent to feel that this is serious business. A projection of serious business at this time is important.

Add Some Humor - Be Loose

A little light humor when you arrive should be easy because you have already gotten into the good graces of the owners, right? If you have not had a chance to meet the sellers, it's no big deal. At this point you should state that your buyers have instructed you not to leave the premises without something signed or the wife will beat you up on the front lawn. Or something to that effect for humor, but *stressing that you intend to leave with some sort of a response.* This is extremely

Larry Hauser

important, and is an integral part of your **SET UP**. It should be your focal point during the entire presentation.

Position Your Opponents Strategically

Like the listing presentation scene, it is important that you do not split the sellers. That is, make sure you don't get in the middle at the table because you are going to be doing a lot of talking and you want to be aware of the reactions of all parties to your sales presentation. Getting to the table should be fairly easy, but once again, make every effort to get this meeting to take place at the kitchen or dining room table.

A very successful tactic I developed over the years was that I would **have the offer in full display on the table, but in a *face down* position on the table.** So, when you arrange yourself at the table, and pull out all of your papers and forms, place the deposit receipt face down on the table just to your left, or your right, but to the side of your note pad.

The Presentation Scene

Now imagine the scene: you are now situated at the table and you are the star of this show. The main actor. All eyes of the audience are on you.

The first thing you should do, providing that you do not have a full priced offer and there are not 5 other agents sitting in the other room waiting their turn to present offers, is that you *mention that your offer is not a full priced offer*, and in fact, your buyers would fall off their chairs if you accepted this offer which you have here! At this point, *tap your hand on the down turned deposit receipt* which is right next to you. However, make sure to state that you have an offer that is a *serious* offer, and what your buyers are interested in doing is purchasing this property for a *"reasonable"* price. Emphasize the word **"reasonable."** Mention that in your years of experience, or months if you are new, you have occasionally run across people

100

who make it clear they want a "steal" and it is your policy to dump these people as politely, but as quickly as possible. You do not have time to work with these people. But your people are interested in paying *"fair market value"* for their home, and that is what you are here tonight to accomplish.

X

Introduction Of Your Buyers

At this point you will present your buyers' credentials in the way of their "Pre-Qualification letter," or a copy of the escrow instructions illustrating the sale of the property they are selling in order to buy this property, or whatever else you might have brought to show the strength of your buyers. Also, a little discussion as to the employment of the buyers, or where they are getting the down payment would certainly be of interest to the sellers, if it had not already been revealed at the "meeting." A little chit chat, ya know.

Regardless, this is the opportunity to "introduce" the financial ability of your buyers to purchase this particular piece of property.

Also, a good thing to interject into the conversation at this point is how your buyers just love the floor plan of this home, or the back yard for their dog, or the schools for their kids, or the fact that it is right next to the race car track, or whatever. Just reinforce the features of this home which your buyers feel are so advantageous to them and therefore, will benefit them over the years.

The Listing Agent's Job Is To *"GET THE DEAL DONE!"*

This should develop into an easy conversation back and forth, and if the other agent is astute, he or she will see the value of this and join in. Hopefully, the other agent will realize that his, or her job, is to **get the deal done**, and not to protect the sellers from some big bad buyers' agent looking to take advantage of their naiveté and congeniality.

While you are talking, make it appear that you are about to turn over the deposit receipt, and thereby reveal the offer price. But don't turn it over - just yet. This will build a little suspense.

How'd You Determine Your Price??

Ask a question, such as, "Oh, by the way, how did you and Mary (their agent) arrive at this asking price for your property, Mr. & Mrs. Jones?" **Whatever the answer, nod your head in the affirmative** and say something like, "It's really difficult to *pinpoint* the *exact* value, isn't it?" Unless you are looking at a brand new, cookie cutter type of property, the answer has to be "yes."

XI

Revealing The Offer Price

It is at this precise time in the presentation that you reveal what your buyers' offer price is. You must do this by **re-stating your earlier statement that your buyers realize that their offer is not one they expect to be accepted**. By this time you should have totally diffused the fact that your offer is not a full-priced offer, because as you have mentioned at least twice, it is not meant to be accepted. *Now*, you turn over the deposit receipt and go over the down payment, loan amount and total "Offer Price."

Quickly Go From Offer Price To Escrow Period, Home Warranty, Etc.

Quickly go into discussion regarding the escrow period, inspection times, home warranty plans, etc., etc., etc., being especially careful to *get agreements to as many of these other items as possible.* By discussing each of the **other** items in the deposit receipt, you are *obtaining acceptance* of your buyers' offer, *excluding the price*, of course.

Bring Out The Counter Offer Form

But, by golly, you've brought a counter offer form with you, (which you flip over at this time) and if you can get a **REASONABLE** number to take back to your buyers, the sellers can sell their home tonight. **"By the way, Mr. & Mrs. Jones, what do you think the real value of your home is?"** As before, wait for an answer. If the other agent isn't a block head, and feels it necessary to do something to verify his value at this time, he won't intervene. Remember, this conversation should be going along in a very easy manner because of all the prep work you have done. Without the prep work, these questions would seem a little forceful on these defenseless sellers.

Don't Argue With The Other Agent

However, if the other agent is the type who must have total control and forgets that his or her job is to **get the deal done**, he may attempt to interject that "numbers" are something they would like to discuss in private. Your response could be something like: "Well, yes, of course, that's fine, but we really are all here for the same thing, so I just thought that if we could get a **"REASONABLE"** number, I could call my buyers right now and get this all agreed upon tonight, doesn't that make some sense?"

Properly Laid Ground Work

Whatever happens at this point, **you have properly laid the ground work for obtaining a reasonable counter-offer**. What I have seen in my many years of making offer presentations to sellers, is that the sellers' representative must feel the necessity to "excuse" you from the table while they talk in private about your offer. I never really understood this, but much of the time it cannot be avoided. Sometimes, when the other agent asked me to leave the room for a short while so that they could "discuss" the offer, I would fake astonishment and say, "Why would you want me to leave? We're all here for the same thing." Sometimes that works, sometimes it doesn't. I have always believed that if both agents were there with the sellers, there would be a better chance of getting a reasonable counter offer based on the true value of the property at that particular time. Some of you will agree with me on this premise, and others, because old habits are hard to change, will not.

It is not always possible to present an offer in this manner. But if you, as the buyers' agent can arrange it, it is beneficial to the entire sales process. If enough **prep work** is done, it doesn't matter what the offer amount is, because you have reinforced that statement several times during the conversation and you can walk away with a "reasonable" counter offer.

The Christmas Eve Presentation

One of my best memories of presenting a low offer on a home happened during the Christmas season a few years ago. As a matter of fact, I had the final counter offer signed at 4:30 in the afternoon on Christmas eve.

Ever Hear Of "Over-Built?"

The subject property was a home in a tract development in Rancho Palos Verdes, California. It was a 4 bedroom home with approximately 2900 square feet and was considerably larger than most other homes in the neighborhood. It also had a black bottomed pool, matching spa, waterfall, sauna, dual air conditioners, 3 patios, unobstructed canyon view, huge family room, all sitting on a huge, 12,600 square foot flat lot, and was offered at $719,000. However, most homes in that tract sold no higher than the high $500,000's. Ever hear of "Over Built?"

This home was so much more expensive than anything else in this area that I had not even previewed it for the buyers I had been working with for the past month. I had no intention of showing them this home, but one morning they called me and told me that they had seen it on the Internet, and wondered why I hadn't shown it to them. I told them that they had told me their top price would be $685,000, and really they wanted to stay around $600,000, and therefore, I had excluded this home from their tour. However, when a buyer asks an agent that question, you have to admit that you feel a little embarrassed, right?

So, I went over and checked it out and was very pleasantly surprised. It was quiet an unusual home. There was excellent quality throughout and it was meticulously decorated in every detail. The Mrs. showed me around and pointed out all the improvements they had made over the last 25 years and that it was quiet an emotional thing, selling this home. She was a very pleasant woman and I did a good warm-up. I made several compliments on the good quality of the improvements. **I got a glass of iced tea out of the deal!**

Problem: "Low Appraisal!"

However, the price still bothered me. So I called the agent, who turned out to be a pretty crafty fellow himself, and was told that the property had been originally offered at $729,000 and they immediately had had two offers and it was sold for $735,000. However, a small problem occurred, which I am sure all of us "seasoned" agents and brokers can relate to: the appraisal came in low. **Thirty Five Thousand Dollars too low!** Well, it seemed that the buyer refused to pay one dollar over the appraised value, and the sellers would not accept a price that low, so it went back on the market - **45 days later!** The other buyer had since purchased another property, and for the next 60 days there was no interest from the market place. A price reduction to $719,000 had not produced any interest, but the agent told me that the sellers would not reduce the price any further at this time. They were emotionally involved in this home, of course.

I fed all of this information to my buyers, a young couple who drove around in a new BMW or SUV, depending on who had the keys for what that day. They had dual incomes and a substantial down payment from the sale of another home in the San Diego area. They had been renting for the past year, so the closing date, or down payment amount were not issues.

Will The Pool Table Fit??

My buyers wanted to see the home, so I made the necessary call to set up the appointment and we went over to take a look. The owners were not home when we arrived, so I just showed them around and I could see that they immediately liked the property. It had most of the things they had been searching for, but we had not been able to locate. When they asked me to get my tape measure to measure the family room to see if their pool table would fit, I knew they were really interested in this home.

Because I had been able to obtain their trust during the previous 3 or 4 weeks, they told me they really did not want to pay more than $700,000 for their home, because that would mean they would have to cut back on their travel and entertainment - definitely serious considerations. In fact, they really did not want to pay more than $685,000, and they asked me if I thought they could get it for that amount. Naturally, I told them that we would never know unless we wrote them an offer, so we went back to my office to talk about it. After pulling the comps from the computer for them to look at, and comparing this house with others we had seen, they agreed that the value of this home was probably pretty close to the appraised amount of $700,000. I discussed with them the value of having buyers meet the sellers of a home, especially if there was a lot of emotion involved with the sellers. They agreed that my idea made some sense.

Getting The Buyers To Meet The Sellers.

So, I contacted the other agent and told him that I was *very close to writing an offer*, but my buyers wanted to ask the sellers a few questions about certain things in the home. He asked me if he could answer the questions and I told him that I thought that perhaps the sellers could tell my buyers enough good things about the neighborhood and the house that perhaps it would help them make their decision.

As I mentioned earlier, this agent was very crafty, and quite experienced, so I am sure he realized that what I was doing couldn't possibly hurt anything. After all, his sellers were very anxious to sell and I was the only game in town at that time.

Later that evening, we all met at the house, and I introduced my young buyers to this couple who were in their late fifties. We snooped around through the home again and then came out to the kitchen (how convenient) and my buyers asked some pre-arranged questions: how are the schools, is it all copper-plumbed, (my favorite, you know), how old is the roof, etc.? Of course, the sellers were ready to talk about their house at any length and a nice rapport was made between the sellers and my buyers. After a short while we left, with the sellers seeing with their own eyes that this couple was actually made up of two human beings who were probably very much like they had been 25 years ago when they had moved into that home.

Writing The Offer

Back at the office, we decided to write an offer for $680,000, with the understanding that they would most certainly have to pay more than that amount if they wanted to buy this house. It was up to me to return with a counter offer which would be acceptable to them.

I called the other agent and asked him if he wouldn't mind making another trip back over to the house so that I could present my offer. He made the call to the sellers and set up the appointment, so an hour later I was back there steering everyone into the kitchen for the presentation. This was not difficult, because the other agent just headed that way and we all followed.

Iced Tea For Everyone!

By this time, I was on a first name basis with the owners, Mike and Barb, and before we sat down she asked if we would like to have some iced tea. SURE! So, it was iced tea all around, as I took out all the paper work and spread it out just according to my plan.

I started by stating that they had had the benefit of seeing that my people were human beings just like they were and that they really liked all the things they had done to the home. I followed that by stating that I had noticed that the home had gone to "Pending" status several months ago and then had come back on the market and that their agent had mentioned to me that the buyer had backed out. Not wanting to reveal that their agent had told me the appraisal problem, I referred to my comps and asked them if it had had anything to do with a low appraisal. She reiterated her agent's statement that the appraisal had come in at $700,000 and that they thought their home was worth more than that. At this point, I realized that the decision maker in this duo was Barb, and that Mike would agree with anything she wanted. (**Sizing Up**)

I brought out the comps, looked them over briefly, and asked her if she had seen them. She looked at them and said that, yes, she had seen them. Looking at all three of them, and then directly at her, I asked her what she thought her home was worth. She quickly replied that she thought it was worth about $715,000, and not a penny less.

Diffusing The Low Offer Price.

At this point, I agreed that her home was certainly the best home in this neighborhood, but unless she could find someone with all cash, another appraisal would probably come in at the same price as before: $700,000. "I certainly don't dispute that price, Barb, because I have seen a lot of houses, but I can tell you that this young couple I am working with can't pay that much for whatever house they finally wind up with. Now, I have an offer here (tapping the over turned deposit receipt) with a substantial down payment and earnest money deposit (looking at the check laying nearby) which we have written up. And, **I can tell you this, if you and Mike were to accept this offer, my people would probably be saying to themselves next week that they could have gotten it for less**. So, they asked me to present this offer knowing that you would counter it. I even brought a counter offer form with me (showing them the counter offer form) which is already for your counter offer, if you wish to make one. They just wanted me to come over with this offer and ask you to give them a ***REASONABLE*** number that they could live with. If I could do that for them, your agent and I can probably put your home in the "**SOLD FILE**" tonight and you and Mike would be on to the next chapter in your lives. *And* your home would be in good hands. (I threw in this last comment because I had sensed that they rather liked my young buyers.)

At this time, I turned over the offer, and pushed a copy to their agent and another towards the sellers. Still talking, I pointed out the down payment and the loan amount, and then the offer price, which in this case was $680,000. **A full $55,000 less than the agreed upon sale price from 3 ½ months earlier!** Do you agree with me that if I had faxed this offer over to the agent, the response would have been less than pleasant? This offer probably would have been looked at as an insult. However, because they could look me right in the eye and hear me say that "This offer is not meant to be accepted," I had a chance to get a reasonable counter offer and, in fact, a chance to accomplish what we were all there for: **to sell the house.**

Fill In The Escrow Period In The Counter

After they had gone over the entire contract, regarding escrow periods, inspections, warranties, etc., I asked her if the escrow period was okay. **THIS QUESTION IS VERY IMPORTANT AT THIS TIME.** If you can get an agreement on the escrow period, you are almost home. In this particular case, they wanted a longer escrow period than my buyers wanted. Remember they were renting. So, what did I do?

Answer: I took the counter-offer form which I had shown them, and had **already filled in the names, times, and addresses**, and wrote in the escrow period. I could have pushed this form to the other agent if I had sensed that he was feeling

---

Larry Hauser

like he was losing control, but as I mentioned, this guy was aware of the duty of the agent: **get the deal done**.

After I filled in the escrow period on the counter offer, I asked her this question: **"Now, concerning price..........................what will you sell your house for tonight to these people?"** My job at that time??? **SHUT UP!** Don't say anything at this point. If they want you to leave so that they can discuss it, don't argue. This is a critical moment. Leave all your stuff there and go into the other room, or out to your car. It doesn't matter. You have done an excellent set up if you have gotten to this point.

All Offers Expire After The Presentation

However, if they ask you if they can have the night to think it over, try your best to get them to work it out before you leave. Tell them that you were instructed by the guy to come back with something written, or he would pummel you in front of your office, or anything you can think of to get something written before you leave. You do not want sellers to have your offer in hand to shop around for something better, even if it is only over night. *That's why I recommend that all offers should be written with the understanding that they expire after the presentation*, and you should emphasize that in the beginning of the meeting, if not sooner. As in your listing presentations, **GET THE SIGNATURES!!** You never know what is going on outside that meeting. If you have successfully presented your buyers as being perfectly capable of buying this home, at a *REASONABLE* selling price, they probably won't want to blow it. Remember, after all of this prep work, you're all "friends" at this point! That's friends with quotation marks ladies and gentlemen, because unless you get the deal, you're nothing. Remember that.

112

"I'll Take $700,000."

In this particular case, Barb, not Mike, said "Write down $700,000." So, I wrote down $700,000, looked at Mike, and said, "Is that okay with you, Mike?" In that order. He just laughed, as did their agent. This *really was* her show. Then I pushed the counter offer towards their agent and asked him if it looked okay. He looked it over and pushed it in their direction for their signatures.

By this time it was about 10:30, and everyone was pretty tired. I phoned my buyers from the other room and told them about the counter offer and that I would need an answer by 5:00 the next day (Christmas Eve). Oddly enough, the escrow period was more of an issue than the price because of the fact that they were renting. However, I can tell you this, if I could have met with those buyers that night, or had been in a hot market, I would have gotten a response that night. If it had been possible, I would have had them *waiting in the car in front of the house*, if I had believed that would have facilitated this deal. If you have gone this far, don't let time get in your way.

They did balk at the price of $700,000, but I told them to think it over and that we would talk about it the next day. I told them to consider the fact that they had looked at approximately 2 dozen homes and that this one, even though it was a bit higher than their "specified" upper limits, fit all their requirements and that they should divide the extra $20,000 in purchase price by the number of years they planned to live in the home. By using this method, they would find the price more "digestible."

The next day, Christmas Eve, they agreed upon the price and at the close of escrow, all parties were happy.

Now, that would be one way of presenting an offer where you are looking to get a counter offer right away. Call it the **"Low Ball Offer"** approach, if you like, but I think you will agree that it is a good way of "working" an offer to a successful conclusion. And believe me, it is WORK.

XII

The "Take It Or Leave It" Offer

Another type of offer presentation which I have found to be successful in a "hot" market is what I call the "**Take It Or Leave It**" offer. When making this type of offer, you must have buyers who will cooperate with you in the fundamentals of the presentation. Of course, you must have the proper qualifications for your buyers to buy this particular piece of property, and you must have them realize that if they want this piece of property, they are going to have to "**step up**," and make a good offer. If your buyers don't realize the quickness of the market for the type of property they are buying, this type of presentation is not going to work and those buyers are probably going to experience disappointment a few times until they realize that you, as the Real Estate agent familiar with the market, is telling the truth when you advise them as to the value of these properties. We have all gone through this routine and sometimes it is necessary before the proper offer can be made.

Make The Offer At "Fair Market" Value.

In order to make this offer, you must have your buyers agree to offer the "fair market value" of the property, or perhaps, a little more. This style of offer is necessary to avoid having your offer used by the other agent to "shop" for a better offer. I spoke earlier of a specific case of "shopping" which was very detrimental to the buyers and their agent. A lot of agents will do this, so you must do all you can to get your offer accepted right at the presentation so that you can avoid having all your efforts turn into a huge amount of wasted time. Remember, half of this instruction manual is dedicated to learning: "*How To Avoid Wasting Time.*"

No FAXes Allowed!

In order to present the "**Take It Or Leave It**" type of offer, it is imperative to present the offer in person. A fax is not going to cut it. A fax is a GIFT to the other agent to allow immediate shopping to begin, many times with their own buyer. So, you must explain to your buyers that you are presenting this offer with the understanding that *you are not to accept any counter offers*. They must be near a telephone when you present the offer, so that you can call and tell them the progress of the offer.

XIII

Ask A Hard Question

As in the previous style of offer presentation, when sitting down at the table with the sellers and their agent, you will lay out your papers on the table with the offer face down. However, the difference here is that you begin your presentation with the statement, "**My client has instructed me to present this offer for signature, or rejection, because he has told me that he is not going to dicker back and forth.** *Is that okay with you?"* Make sure that you include the second part of that question: "Is that okay with you?" Now, that is a **HARD question** to put before these sellers, and usually they do not care to be put on the spot like that. Therefore, you will be required to explain to these people that your buyer is the type of individual who does not want to waste time. You have his "financial credentials" and a pre-qualification letter, and that the offer is at a "fair market" price. "If you, Mr. & Mrs. Jones, would like to sell your property tonight, you can do it if you like this offer."

No Need For A "Warm-Up" Here.

There is no need for a "warm-up" with this type of offer. This is strictly business, and that is what you are there for. You don't need a glass of water and you don't have to comment on what a great picture that is of Elvis hanging over the couch. You should be dressed accordingly: guys, dress shirt and tie; ladies, business attire. It is very important to project the business image here. This is probably the first time these sellers have seen you, so remember what I said earlier about first impressions.

Now, this type of abrupt offer style may be offensive to some agents and to some sellers. However, if you are congenial, and *"loose,"* and explain to them that you are only doing it in this manner because you were instructed to do so by your "business-like" buyer, the harshness is directed away from you. It is your job, as a **SALES** person, to sell this offer and to get the signatures. If your offer is not high enough to suit the sellers, do your best to get them to agree that your offer, being based on comparable sales which you have brought along for the occasion, is a "fair market" offer. Sometimes the sellers' expectations from the market place are much higher than the actual value of their property and, if enough time has not passed with the property being in the MLS, your *realistic* offer is not going to fly anyway.

Stand Firm!

Regardless, you must stand firm on the fact that your offer is not to be countered. However, if they insist on a counter anyway, you must call your client, right then and there and allow the other agent to hear him say "**Rejected**" before you leave the table. **Do not, under any circumstances, leave your offer in their hands when you leave unless they have written "Rejected" across the first page!!** This step is extremely important and if followed correctly, will save you pain, frustration, and TIME! If they have elected, against your recommendation, to counter your offer, and they have heard your client say "Rejected" on the phone, you still have room to play.

Remember, you are a **SALES** person and this is your game. So, after you hang up the phone with your client, begin to pack up your papers, and then, like in the *"Columbo Close,"* stop what you are doing and look the sellers right in the eye and ask, "**By the way, Mr. & Mrs. Jones, is there any way I can get you to reconsider your position on your counter offer?** Perhaps, if you could make your price a little closer to my buyers' offer price, I could meet with him tomorrow and hammer him over the head with it a little bit. Who knows, he might be willing to pay a little more than what he has offered?" If you can get them to give you a better counter offer, you can leave with *something*! If you can do that, the ball is back in your hands and you have allowed yourself a chance to "sell" your buyer the property. Does that sound like it makes sense?

And if you cannot get the seller to reconsider his counter offer, at minimum you will have gained information for your buyer as to what they will take for the property. He will have the opportunity to mull over this information and decide whether he wants to go that high, or if he wants to wait for another property to come on the market. If he decides, after thinking about it overnight, or for a few days, that he will pay that higher amount, write up another offer and present it in the same manner. That is, if the property is still available.

Either way, you either get the deal, or you don't. But you have **not** left an open offer in the hands of the listing agent so that your competition can come in and beat you out by $500. This is a tough way to present an offer, but if you prepare yourself to be tough, you will get the deal.

Ah! You are probably asking yourself, "What if the sellers elect to reject the offer? What then?"

Indeed. What then? Apparently, your efforts to this point have been for naught for you will be walking out of the meeting with nothing. But, as I mentioned at the beginning of this strategy, you either get the deal, or you don't. In this case, you don't get the deal, but you have also left the sellers with nothing as well. They do not have the power to show your "Open Offer" to any other potentially interested parties, and therefore, they are back at square one. If they are asking an unrealistic price for their property, they will be required to wait until the market reaches their expectations, which may be never, or they will be thinking in a few days, or less, that perhaps your offer was a pretty good offer after all. Has anyone in the Real Estate business ever seen something like that happen to sellers with over priced properties? Yes, indeedy.

IT'S MORE WORK - THAT'S FOR SURE.

Is this more work? YES! But why *not* do this additional work to better enhance your chance of getting an offer accepted? You have worked very hard to get to this point. Why not make it your *Standard Operational Procedure* to do it 100%? Why not do everything possible to improve your chances of being paid for the work you do? Remember, you are COMMISSION sales people. You earn nothing until you get the deal.

Multiple Offers

In a hot market, many times you will find yourself in a position where you are "standing in line" to present your offer. This can be exasperating and the result is always the same: only one agent is going to get the deal. So, how can you, the Real Estate professional, improve your chances of having your offer selected from the several on the table in front of the seller?

The first thing you must accomplish in this situation is the preparation of your buyers. If they do not understand that they are going to be competing against other buyers for this property, than they are going to suffer disappointment. And you will suffer WASTED TIME. We all know that this might be unavoidable because much of the time buyers must "lose" a house before they finally buy one. Most of the time it is because they do not believe their agent when they are "coached" on what to offer on the home. They may have had a call from their Uncle Louie in Horse Pasture, Virginia who advises them not to go in too high. He bought a house once about 35 years ago and he definitely knows that you can't trust the Real Estate agents because all they want is to make the deal. It is very difficult to overcome that obstacle, and it may *require* that the buyers miss a few before they are ready to listen to your good advise and step up to the line.

However, when your buyers realize that it will be difficult to get their offer accepted in a busy market, there are ways in which

119

you, the *trained* salesperson, can have an advantage over your competitors.

They Better Be Qualified.

If you have not had your buyers pre-qualified for this transaction, you are going about your business backwards. No seller, or sellers' agent, will even consider an offer in a hot market from buyers who have not been pre-qualified. It would even be better if you could have your buyers pre-APPROVED for the loan necessary to close this transaction. Pre-approval takes longer to obtain from the lender and therefore, may not be possible if you have just started working with these people. You should start towards that pre-approval as soon as possible. It is a strong point to include with your offer.

However, with a pre-qualification letter, and buyers that are properly "prepped" to make a strong offer, you must know the strategy which will best enhance your chances of having your buyers get the deal.

With a scenario such that you know there will probably be over-bids on the property, you must discuss with your buyers the probability that the home will be sold at a price more than the asking price. If they really want the home, and are qualified to pay more, you must discuss with them how much over the asking price they are willing to pay. It is not necessary to go in with that "maximum" offer price in writing, but a discussion with the sellers, or the agent, must be made either at the presentation, or just beforehand. Do not give up the "top" price your buyers are willing to pay, because then, most likely, the sellers will ask for a little more. The old "G" factor comes into play with sellers who have several offers on the table in front of them.

Usually what happens in situations where there are several offers on a property is that the sellers and their agent select one or two, or sometimes three offers, and they counter those with the phrase, "Buyer to submit highest and best offer by such and such time and date." This will usually weed out those who really want the property from those who still must learn that they must "step up to the plate," so to speak.

But how can you get the deal for your buyers?

How about this: "Buyer agrees to pay $500 (or $1,000, or whatever) more than the highest bidder up to a maximum of $XXX,XXX." Does that sound like cheating? Maybe it is, but it is not written anywhere that I have ever seen where that type of response is illegal. How did I learn this? By experience. I lost a deal in this manner when I learned of the phrase which aced me out on an offer on a property in Torrance, CA in 1988. I had a connection with an escrow officer, who shall remain un-named for obvious reasons, who did the escrow on that transaction and told me how the buyers' agent had worded the counter to the counter offer. I couldn't **BELIEVE** that I had lost that deal for only $1,000 on a $350,000 property! Another lesson learned which cost me about $7,500 in commissions. It's always expensive to make a mistake in the Real Estate business, I am sure you'll agree.

If you learn how to operate in this situation, you may save yourself from this costly mistake. Of course, it doesn't always work. For example, your buyers may be restricted in their maximum amount and one of the other buyers may get the property with a higher bid, but you *will* have the advantage if you use this method in those occasional busy markets.

Larry Hauser

CONCLUSION

In conclusion, I would like to make a few comments about the Real Estate business in general.

Don't Talk Yourself Out Of The Deal.

First, I have noticed that too many agents, after they have developed some degree of success, seem to become too much in love with themselves and often "talk" themselves out of deals. When you are receiving an offer on one of your listings and the offer price is not where you think it should be, it is sometimes tempting to tell your seller that he can get more. **It is not your job at this point to tell your seller what he can get for his property.** It is your job to "generate" offers from the market place. Perhaps your seller *can* get more for the property. But if you have an offer on the table, and there are no others waiting to be presented by agents sitting in the other room, what you have in front of you is "*one of a kind.*"

Don't Play "Mother Hen."

Do not be tempted into playing the "mother hen." At this point, you should confer with your sellers about the *good points* of the offer, and then review the comparable sales with them. You should play a professorial role with your clients at this point, and inform them that it is *their decision* as to what to do with this offer. How many times have we "advised" our clients that the offer on the table was "way too low" and then tell them what price to counter? Then that buyer goes away and 3 months later the property is still on the market with no other offers in between. You know what happens then: the listing expires and they list with Suzie at Sea Breeze Realty at $10,000 less and it sells in one week. Has that ever happened to anyone reading this book? I have lost a few like that myself when I was new in the business. Remember your position in the equation: as listing agent, or buying agent, your job is to get the property ***SOLD!*** It is much easier to tell your clients at the end of the listing period that their decision to counter that first offer at such a high number was probably not a good idea and that you would recommend such and such as a new, reduced asking price. Does that make any sense to anybody?

Don't Condescend To Your Fellow Agents.

Another point I would like to make before ending is that I have seen a lot of agents become condescending to those who have not reached their level yet. Perhaps they have a listing, or several listings, and suddenly agents working with buyers aren't as good as they are. Perhaps, an offer is made on one of their listings which is not perfect in every way, and they express annoyance at the agent presenting the offer. Has anyone ever experienced a situation like this? Well, so have I and I can tell you, it can be very irritating. Always remember, if you have a listing, you really don't have anything except an obligation to advertise that listing and listen to your seller scream at you because the property isn't sold. So, unless you have a buyer for that listing, you don't have anything.

Be Helpful To Your Fellow Agent.

I would recommend that you always treat your fellow agent with respect, and if necessary, help him or her, with the offer. It will make you feel good by doing that and the word will get around that you are nice to work with. Remember, everyone is not as smart as you are, so it shows a virtue if you can help people who don't know the ropes as well as you do. And there are a lot of new agents in the Real Estate business who will learn the basics of the business over time. And if you are a new agent, it should not be taboo to inform the agent on the other side that you *are* new and that perhaps you might need a little help with the deal. **Always remember that your position as the *agent* is to get the deal done.** Every offer that comes in is not going to be perfect, and it is the job of the agents to work it out so that both sides are satisfied. That's why we're all rich - because we can work out the little details that can blow the deals.

Salesmanship Is Simply *"Persuasion."*

So, I would like to conclude with this final thought. The entire theme of this book is that in order to improve yourself in the Real Estate business and cut down on time wasted, you must become trained in the skill, or art if you will, of salesmanship. And salesmanship is nothing more than "persuasion." Persuading people to *think your way*. Practice talking to people in the F.A.B. manner. Remember, you are selling an expensive product. Sometimes it's a home. Sometimes its an income property. Always, it's you!

Your Presentations Are Actually *"Performances."*

And when you make your presentations with a prepared plan, *written and rehearsed*, you will have the advantage over your competition AND your prospects. After a while, you won't need a written plan because you will have *"performed"* so many times it will become your natural way of *"selling."* Like the actor on the stage, after a while, the lines are memorized and the actor "becomes" that character. Does that make some sense? Do you see how this can help you?

Thank you taking the effort to improve yourself in the field of selling. I hope that I have provided you with some tools which will help you become more successful, and at the same time more fully enjoy the occupation you have chosen for yourselves.

Good luck in selling.

ABOUT THE AUTHOR

Larry Hauser began his career in selling at the age of 13. His first "commission" job was selling Christmas cards in Ocean City, New Jersey. It was in those first few weeks that he realized that he was born to sell. And it was also at this early age, with this door to door sales job, that he discovered for himself that certain techniques worked better than others in arriving at what every sales person searches for: signatures on the bottom line.

After college he knew that some type of sales job had to be his way of life. He experienced sales jobs with a large life insurance company, a major magazine publisher, and one of the leading providers of long term health care insurance before finding his true love in the Real Estate business.

Over the years he developed certain sales strategies which provided him with advantages over his competitors who were not trained as **"Sales"** people. These strategies are made available in this, his first publication, *"The Complete Guide To Success In Real Estate Sales."*

For those who have asked themselves, "How much money have I left on the table by not asking the right questions," this book is a must-read. Call it a training manual, a sales manual, or simply a good idea, those who are interested in saving themselves time and money in their chosen profession must take time to read his book. If you are serious about yourself in the field of Real Estate Sales, you owe it to yourself to thoroughly understand and practice his selling strategies.

CONTACT THE AUTHOR

For Information Regarding Sales Training By The Author

www.lunadases.com